Comprehensive Conservation Plan

North Dakota Limited-interest
National Wildlife Refuges

April 2006

Prepared by the U.S. Fish and Wildlife Service

U.S. Fish and Wildlife Service, Region 6
Division of Refuge Planning
PO Box 25486 DFC
Lakewood, CO 80225
303/236 4370

Approved by:

4/14/06

_____   _____
J. Mitch King   Date
Regional Director, Region 6
U.S. Fish and Wildlife Service
Lakewood, CO

Comprehensive Conservation Plan Approval

North Dakota Limited-interest National Wildlife Refuges

Submitted by:

_____ 4/6/06

Kim Hanson   Date
Project Leader
Arrowwood National Wildlife Refuge Complex
Pingree, ND

_____ 4/6/06

Lloyd Jones   Date
Project Leader
Audubon National Wildlife Refuge Complex
Coleharbor, ND

_____ 4/11/06

Roger Hollevoet   Date
Project Leader
Devils Lake Wetland Management District
Devils Lake, ND

_____ 4/6/06

Tedd Gutzke   Date
Project Leader
J. Clark Salyer National Wildlife Refuge Complex
Upham, ND

_____ 4/6/06

Mick Erickson   Date
Project Leader
Kulm Wetland Management District
Kulm, ND

_____ 4/6/06

Paul Van Ningen   Date
Project Leader
Long Lake National Wildlife Refuge Complex
Moffit, ND

Concurred with:

_____ 4/12/06

Rod Krey   Date
Refuge Program Supervisor (ND, SD)
U.S. Fish and Wildlife Service, Region 6
Lakewood, CO

_____ 4/12/06

Richard A. Coleman, Ph.D.   Date
Assistant Regional Director
National Wildlife Refuge System
U.S. Fish and Wildlife Service, Region 6
Lakewood, CO

North Dakota Limited-interest National Wildlife Refuges

Appert Lake
Ardoch
Bone Hill
Brumba
Buffalo Lake
Camp Lake
Canfield Lake
Cottonwood Lake
Dakota Lake
Half Way Lake
Hiddenwood
Hobart Lake
Hutchinson Lake
Johnson Lake
Lake George
Lake Otis
Lake Patricia
Lambs Lake
Little Goose
Lords Lake

Lost Lake
Maple River
Pleasant Lake
Pretty Rock
Rabb Lake
Rock Lake
Rose Lake
School Section Lake
Sheyenne Lake
Sibley Lake
Silver Lake
Snyder Lake
Springwater
Stoney Slough
Sunburst Lake
Tomahawk
Willow Lake
Wintering River
Wood Lake

Abbreviations Used in this CCP

BMPs	best management practices
BOR	Bureau of Reclamation
CCP	comprehensive conservation plan
EA	environmental assessment
EO	executive order
FmHA Lands	Farmers Home Administration Lands
FONSI	finding of no significant impact
HAPET	"Habitat and Population Evaluation Team"
Improvement Act	National Wildlife Refuge System Improvement Act of 1997
NDGF	North Dakota Game and Fish Department
NEPA	National Environmental Policy Act of 1969
NWR	national wildlife refuge
Program	"North Dakota Limited-interest Refuge Program"
Service	U.S. Fish and Wildlife Service
System	National Wildlife Refuge System
USFWS	U.S. Fish and Wildlife Service
WMA	wildlife management area
WMD	wetland management district
WPA	waterfowl production area

(See "Appendix B, Glossary of Terms" and "Appendix D, Key Legislation and Policies" for further terms and descriptions.)

Contents

Tables

Figures

Chapter 1. Introduction

The U.S. Fish and Wildlife Service (Service) has developed this comprehensive conservation plan (CCP) to provide a foundation for the management and use of 39 limited-interest national wildlife refuges located primarily throughout eastern North Dakota. The CCP is intended as a working guide for management programs and actions over the next 15 years.

The CCP was developed in compliance with the National Wildlife Refuge System Improvement Act of 1997 (Improvement Act) and Part 602 (National Wildlife Refuge System Planning) of the Fish and Wildlife Service Manual. The actions described within this CCP also meet the requirements of the National Environmental Policy Act of 1969 (NEPA). Compliance with NEPA is being achieved through the involvement of the public and the inclusion of an integrated environmental assessment (EA).

When fully implemented, this CCP will strive to achieve the North DakotaLimited-interest Refuge Program (Program) vision and the purposes of each refuge. Fish and wildlife are the first priority in refuge management, and public use (wildlife-dependent recreation) is allowed and encouraged as long as permission is granted by the affected landowners and it is compatible with, or does not detract from a refuge's purpose(s).

The CCP has been prepared by a planning team composed of representatives from various Service programs, including Refuges and Realty, and the North Dakota Game and Fish Department (NDGF). In developing this plan, the planning team has incorporated the input of the landowners who own most of these refuge lands and local citizens and organizations. This public involvement and the planning process itself are described in section 1.5, "The Planning Process."

After reviewing a wide range of public comments and management needs, the planning team developed the preferred alternative. This action will attempt to address all significant issues while determining how best to achieve the intent and purposes of the Program. The preferred alternative is the Service's recommended course of action for the future management of these refuges, and is embodied in this CCP.

1.1 Purpose and Need for Plan

The purpose of this CCP is to identify the role that the Program will play in support of the mission of the National Wildlife Refuge System (System), and to provide long-term guidance for managing refuge programs and activities. The CCP is needed:

- To build relationships with the landowners and communicate with the general public and other partners in efforts to carry out the mission of the System.
- To provide a clear statement of direction for the future management of the Program;
- To provide landowners, neighbors, visitors, and government officials with an understanding of the U.S. Fish and Wildlife Service's management actions on and around these refuges;
- To ensure that the Service's management actions are consistent with the mandates of the Improvement Act;
- To ensure that the management of these refuges is consistent with federal, state, and county plans; and
- To provide a basis for the development of budget requests for the Program's operation, maintenance, and capital improvement needs.

Sustaining our Nation's fish and wildlife resources is a task that can be accomplished only through the combined efforts of governments, businesses, and private citizens.

1.2 The U.S. Fish and Wildlife Service and the National Wildlife Refuge System

The U.S. Fish and Wildlife Service

The mission of the U.S. Fish and Wildlife Service, working with others, is to conserve, protect, and enhance fish and wildlife and their habitats for the continuing benefit of the American people.

Over a hundred years ago, America's fish and wildlife resources were declining at an alarming rate. Concerned citizens, scientists, and hunting and angling groups joined together to restore and sustain our national wildlife heritage. This was the genesis of the U.S. Fish and Wildlife Service.

Today, the Service enforces federal wildlife laws, manages migratory bird populations, restores nationally significant fisheries, conserves and restores vital wildlife habitat, protects and recovers endangered species, and helps other governments with conservation efforts. It also administers a federal aid program that distributes hundreds of millions of dollars to states for fish and wildlife restoration, boating access, hunter education, and related programs across America.

The Service is the managing agency of the Program along with the rest of the System, thousands of waterfowl production areas (WPA), and other special management areas. It also operates 66 national fish hatcheries and 78 ecological services field stations.

Service Activities in North Dakota

Service activities in North Dakota contribute to the state's economy, ecosystems, and education programs. The following lists the Service's presence and activities in North Dakota, reported in 2005:

- The Service employs 201 people.
- Over 14,245 hours were donated by 623 volunteers to help Service projects.
- There are two national fish hatcheries and one fish and wildlife management assistance office.
- Sixty-five national wildlife refuges encompass 342,799 acres (0.8 percent of the state).

- There are 12 wetland management districts.
  - Fee waterfowl production areas cover 284,317 acres (0.6 percent of the state).
  - There are 1,046,358 wetland acres (2.4 percent of the state) under various leases or easements, including these limited-interest refuges.
- Service-managed lands hosted more than 394,063 visitors—
  - 152,160 hunting visits
  - 142,281 wildlife observation visits
  - 83,650 fishing visits
  - 2,360 trapping visits
  - Over 51,000 students participated in environmental education programs.
- The Service provided $3.8 million to NDGF for sport fish restoration and $3.4 million for wildlife restoration and hunter education.
- Since 1987, the Partners for Wildlife program has helped private landowners restore over 21,008 acres on 3,351 sites and 170,217 acres on 1,113 sites; and 47.8 miles of river.
  - The Service employs 11 program managers for Partners for Wildlife in the state.
- The Service paid North Dakota counties more than $852,271 under the Refuge Revenue Sharing Act; funds were used for schools and roads.

The National Wildlife Refuge System

In 1903, President Theodore Roosevelt designated the 5.5-acre Pelican Island in Florida as the nation's first wildlife refuge for the protection of brown pelicans and other native nesting birds. This was the first time the federal government set aside land for the sake of wildlife. This small but significant designation was the beginning of the System. One hundred years later, this System has become the largest collection of lands in the world specifically managed for wildlife, encompassing over 96 million acres within 544 refuges and over 3,000 small areas for waterfowl breeding and nesting. Today, there is at least one refuge in every state in the nation including Puerto Rico and the U.S. Virgin Islands.

In 1997, a clear mission was established for the System through the passage of the Improvement Act. That mission is:

to administer a national network of lands and waters for the conservation, management, and where appropriate, restoration of the fish, wildlife and plant resources and their habitats within the United States for the benefit of present and future generations of Americans.

The Improvement Act further states that each refuge shall be managed:

- to fulfill the mission of the System;
- to fulfill the individual purposes of each refuge;
- to consider the needs of fish and wildlife first;
- to fulfill the requirement of developing a CCP for each unit of the System, and fully involve the public in the preparation of these plans;
- to maintain the biological integrity, diversity, and environmental health of the System;
- to recognize that wildlife-dependent recreation activities including hunting, fishing, wildlife observation, wildlife photography, and environmental education and interpretation, are legitimate and priority public uses; and
- to retain the authority of refuge managers to determine compatible public uses.

In addition to the overall mission for the System, the wildlife and habitat vision for each national wildlife refuge stresses the following principles:

- Wildlife comes first.
- Ecosystems, biodiversity, and wilderness are vital concepts in refuge management.
- Refuges must be healthy.
- Growth of refuges must be strategic.
- The System serves as a model for habitat management with broad participation from others.

Following passage of the Improvement Act, the Service immediately began efforts to carry out

the direction of the new legislation, including the preparation of CCPs for all refuges. The development of these plans is now ongoing nationally. Consistent with the Improvement Act, all refuge CCPs are being prepared in conjunction with public involvement, and each refuge is required to complete its own CCP within the 15-year schedule (by 2012).

People and the National Wildlife Refuge System

Our fish and wildlife heritage contributes to the quality of our lives and is an integral part of our nation's greatness. Wildlife and wild places have always given people special opportunities to have fun, relax, and appreciate our natural world.

Whether through bird watching, fishing, hunting, photography, or other wildlife pursuits, wildlife recreation also contributes millions of dollars to local economies. In 2002, approximately 35.5 million people visited a national wildlife refuge, mostly to observe wildlife in their natural habitats. Visitors are most often accommodated through nature trails, auto tours, interpretive programs and hunting and fishing opportunities. Significant economic benefits are being generated to the local communities that surround the refuges. Economists have reported that national wildlife refuge visitors contribute more than $792 million annually to local economies.

1.3 National and Regional Mandates

Refuges are managed to achieve the mission and goals of the System and the designated purpose of the refuge unit as described in establishing legislation or executive orders, or other establishing documents. Key concepts and guidance of the System are provided in the Refuge System Administration Act of 1966 (P.L. 87-714), Title 50 of the Code of Federal Regulations, the Fish and Wildlife Service Manual and, most recently, through the Improvement Act.

The Improvement Act amends the Refuge System Administration Act by providing a unifying mission for the System, a new process for determining compatible public uses on refuges, and a requirement that each refuge will be managed under a CCP. The Improvement Act states that wildlife conservation is the priority of System lands and that the Secretary of the Interior will ensure that the biological integrity, diversity and environmental health of refuge lands are maintained. Each refuge must be managed to fulfill the System's mission and the specific purposes for which it was established. The Improvement Act requires the Service to monitor the status and trends of fish, wildlife, and plants in each refuge. A list of other laws and executive orders that may affect the CCP or the Service's implementation of the CCP is provided in "Appendix D, Key Legislation and Policies." Service policies providing guidance on planning and the day-to-day management of a refuge are contained within the Refuge System Manual and the Service Manual.

1.4 Ecosystem Descriptions and Threats

Mississippi Headwaters–Tallgrass Prairie Ecosystem

Thirty-three refuges in this Program are located east of the Missouri River within the Mississippi Headwaters–Tallgrass Prairie Ecosystem. This ecosystem is primarily located in Minnesota, South Dakota, and North Dakota with small sections extending into Wisconsin and Iowa. This ecosystem encompasses a major portion of the Prairie Pothole Region of North America. The Prairie Pothole Region produces 20 percent of the continental waterfowl populations annually.

Historically, this portion of North America was subject to periodic glaciation; glacial meltwaters were instrumental in forming the five major river systems located or partly located within this ecosystem. These river systems are: Mississippi, St. Croix, Red, Missouri, and Minnesota. Likewise, glacial moraines and other deposits resulted in a myriad of lakes and wetlands common throughout this area. Significant variation in the topography and soils of the area attest to the ecosystem's dynamic glacial history.

The three major ecological communities within this ecosystem are the tallgrass prairie, the northern boreal forest, and the eastern deciduous forest. Grasses common to the tallgrass prairie include big bluestem, little bluestem, Indian grass, sideoats grama, and switch grass. Native tallgrass prairie also supports ecologically important forbs such as prairie cone flower, purple prairie clover, and blazing star. The northern boreal forest ecological community comprises a variety of

coniferous species such as jack pine, balsam fir, and spruce. Common tree species in the eastern deciduous forest ecological community include maple, basswood, red oak, white oak, and ash. Current land uses range from tourism and timber industries in the northern forests to intensive agriculture in the historic tallgrass prairie. Of the three major ecological communities, the tallgrass prairie is the most threatened with more than 99 percent of it having been converted for agricultural purposes.

Due to its ecological and vegetative diversity, the Mississippi Headwaters–Tallgrass Prairie Ecosystem supports at least 121 species of neotropical migrants and other migratory birds. It provides breeding and migration habitat for significant populations of waterfowl plus a variety of other waterbirds. The ecosystem supports several species of candidate and federally listed threatened and endangered species including the bald eagle, piping plover, Higgins eye pearly mussel, Karner blue butterfly, prairie bush clover, Leedy's roseroot, dwarf trout lily, and the western prairie fringed orchid. The increasingly rare paddlefish and lake sturgeon are also found in portions of this ecosystem.

There has been no prior planning or establishment of headwaters focus areas in the Mississippi Headwaters–Tallgrass Prairie Ecosystem.

Hudson Bay Ecosystem (part of the Missouri Main Stem River Ecosystem)

Lake Patricia and Pretty Rock National Wildlife Refuges are located within a portion of the Missouri Main Stem River Ecosystem identified as the Hudson Bay Ecosystem. This ecosystem includes portions of the Missouri River and Hudson Bay watersheds. An initial Ecosystem Management Plan developed by the Ecosystem Team identified four focus areas needing the highest priority for protection and evaluation; wetlands, the Missouri River, native prairies, and riparian areas. Priorities were based on significance in the ecosystem, species diversity, risk and/or threat to the entire focus area, public benefits, international values, and trust resources. Although a detailed analysis of habitats, threats, and priorities for this ecosystem has not been completed, a vision and set of goals and objectives have been developed for each of these focus areas. The overall threats and visions for each focus area include:

Wetlands

Threats: The glaciated prairies on North and South Dakota and northeastern Montana cover approximately 60 million acres. Once a myriad of prairie pothole wetlands in a sea of native prairie, the area is now the "bread basket" of the country and intensively farmed. Drainage, for agricultural purposes has reduced 7.2 million acres of wetlands by over 40 percent to 3.9 million acres.

Vision: Diverse, wetland habitats and watersheds that provide an abundance and diversity of native flora and fauna in the ecosystem for the benefit of the American public.

Missouri River

Threats: The Missouri River is vastly different from the "untamed" flood plain system of even 50 years ago. Originating in the Rocky Mountains of south-central Montana, the river flows 2,300 miles, traversing seven states and passing through seven mainstem dams built and maintained by the federal government. Over 900 miles (nearly 60 percent) of the former upper river passing through Montana, North Dakota, South Dakota, and Nebraska now lie under permanent multi-purpose reservoirs. As the Missouri River changed, so did the wildlife communities that depend on it. Currently 8 fishes, 15 birds, 6 mammals, 4 reptiles, 6 insects, 4 mollusks, and 7 plants native to the ecosystem are listed as either threatened or endangered or are under status review for possible listing.

Vision: A healthy Missouri River capable of self-sustaining fish and wildlife resources.

Native Prairie

Threats: Native Prairie in the Missouri Main Stem River Ecosystem consists of tall grass, mid-grass, and short grass prairies from the eastern Dakotas to the west. Although the plant and wildlife species differ across the gradation from tall to short grass, the threats and issues remain the same—conversion of prairie to other uses. The west river area of North Dakota has lost approximately 60 percent of the original 34 million acres of native prairie due to agricultural conversion.

Vision: Protect, restore and maintain ecosystem native prairie and other grasslands to ensure its diversity and abundance of native flora and fauna.

Riparian Areas

Threats: Riparian areas make up a small portion of the habitat in the Hudson Bay (Missouri Main Stem River) Ecosystem. However, riparian and riverine wetland habitats are more important than other focus areas to fish and wildlife resources including migratory birds, threatened and endangered species, native fish, rare and declining fisheries, amphibians and many mammals. Riparian habitats provide for much of the biodiversity in the ecosystem. Many of the species currently occurring in the ecosystem would be eliminated without healthy riparian areas. Sedimentation, contamination, invasive species, and development threaten the health of this diverse habitat.

Vision: Healthy riparian and flood plain ecosystems that provide an abundance and diversity of indigenous flora and fauna.

1.5 The Planning Process

This CCP and EA for the 39 limited-interest refuges and the Program are intended to comply with the Improvement Act, NEPA, and the implementing regulations of the acts. The Service issued a final refuge planning policy in 2000 that established requirements and guidance for System planning, including CCPs and step-down management plans, ensuring that planning efforts comply with the provisions of the Improvement Act. The planning policy identified several steps of the CCP and EA process (see figure 1):

- Form a planning team and conduct pre-planning (see "Appendix A, Consultation and Coordination")
- Initiate public involvement and scoping
- Draft vision statement and goals
- Develop and analyze alternatives, including the preferred alternative
- Prepare draft CCP and EA
- Prepare and adopt final CCP and EA and issue a finding of no significant impact (FONSI) or determine if an environmental impact statement is needed.
- Implement CCP, monitor and evaluate

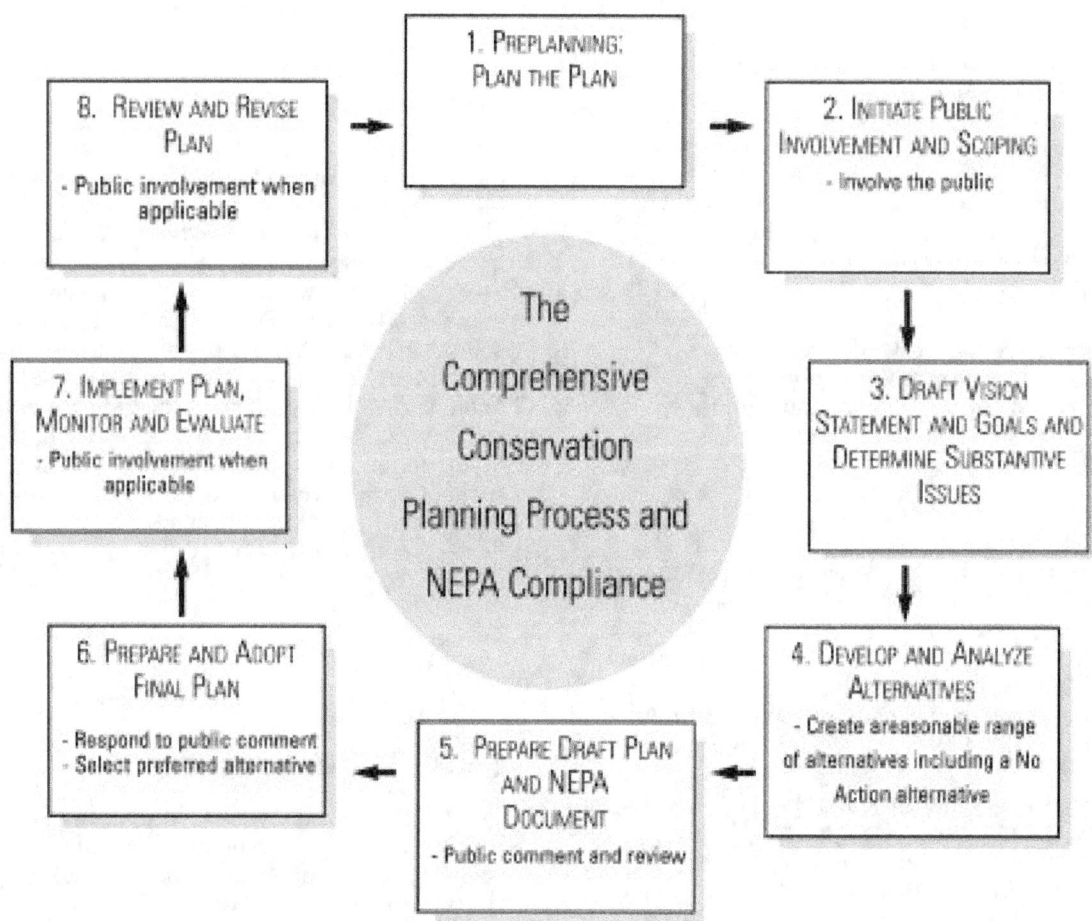

Figure 1. The steps in the CCP process

■   Review every 5 years and revise CCP every 15 years

This is a dynamic process that may require revisiting various steps. Nevertheless, the first step to developing this Program was determining the criteria for including limited-interest refuges in this CCP. Although there are other limited-interest refuges in North Dakota and other states, including South Dakota and Montana, the 39 refuges covered in the CCP were selected based on the following criteria:

■   Refuge is located within North Dakota
■   Less than 15 percent of the refuge acres are fee-title national wildlife refuge acres, the remainder are in private ownership or are WPAs.

Refuges with significant amounts of fee-title NWR acres were excluded from this CCP based on their significantly greater management capabilities. These refuges will be addressed in separate planning efforts. The WPAs within and adjacent to these refuge boundaries will be addressed in future WMD CCPs for the managing station.

The Service began the pre-planning process in December 2003. A planning team of Service personnel from each of the six managing stations, Division of Realty and Refuges, and NDGF, was developed shortly after an initial kickoff meeting. Draft issues and qualities were developed and updated over a course of several meetings. During pre-planning, several items were addressed including developing a mailing list and determining the rights the Service purchased with the limited-interest refuge agreements.

Over the course of pre-planning and scoping, the planning team collected available information about the resources of the limited-interest refuges and the surrounding areas. This information is summarized under "Chapter 4, Affected Environment."

Due to the number of refuges in this planning effort, this CCP became more of a programmatic CCP than the more traditional management CCP. This CCP provides long-term guidance for management decisions; sets forth goals, objectives, and strategies needed to accomplish refuge purposes; and identifies the Service's best estimate of future needs.

This CCP details Program planning levels that are sometimes substantially above current budget allocations and, as such, are primarily for Service strategic planning purposes. This CCP does not constitute a commitment for staffing increases, operational and maintenance increases, or funding for future land acquisition.

Public scoping began in March 2004 with the initial contact of the 225 refuge landowners. A Notice of Intent to prepare and EA was published in the Federal Register on July 2, 2004.

Coordination with the Landowners and Other Publics

The planning team ensured that the first stakeholders to be contacted during scoping were landowners of limited-interest refuges. A mailing list of over 225 names was created and included private citizens, the North Dakota State Land and Game and Fish Departments, and the Bureau of Reclamation (BOR). In May 2004, a personal letter was sent to each landowner introducing them to the CCP process and providing history on the Program. Each was invited to participate in the process and to offer comments. The initial response was minimal. In early July 2004, a newsletter was mailed to each landowner and over 460 additional individuals and organizations (over 700 total). Information was provided on the history of the Program and the CCP process along with a schedule of and invitation to upcoming open houses. Open houses also were announced in 37 local newspapers.

A total of 19 open houses were held between July 14, 2004 and September 16, 2004. At the start of each meeting, the CCP planner or the refuge personnel gave a presentation on the history of the Program along with an overview of the CCP/NEPA process. Attendees were encouraged to ask questions and offer comments. Attendees were invited to submit additional thoughts or questions in writing and each was given a two-page comment form to complete. The turnout was mixed, from no attendees to 19 individuals at a single-refuge meeting. In addition to scoping meetings, postage-paid comment forms were sent to everyone on the mailing list (over 700 individuals), with a September 30 response deadline. Forty-six written comments were received. Input obtained from all of these meetings and correspondence was considered in developing this CCP.

State Coordination

The North Dakota Game and Fish Department's mission is to "protect, conserve, and enhance fish and wildlife populations and their habitats for sustained public consumptive and nonconsumptive uses." Overall, the NDGF is responsible for managing natural resource lands owned by the state in addition to enforcement responsibilities for the state's migratory birds and endangered species resources. The state currently manages over 78,000 acres in support of wildlife, recreation, and fisheries.

In January 2004, an invitation letter to participate in the CCP process was sent by the Region 6 regional director to the Director of the NDGF. Local NDGF wildlife managers and the refuge staffs maintain excellent and ongoing working relations that precede the start of the CCP process. An NDGF representative is part of the core CCP planning team and has been participating in most of the workshops. In addition to the NDGF, all relative federal, state (see below), and county representatives, including all county chairpersons, were provided a newsletter introducing them to this Program and welcoming their comments.

Elected officials were initially contacted by the North Dakota Refuge Coordinator by telephone and mail about the CCP in January 2004. They were contacted again through a newsletter that outlined the public scoping meeting schedule.

The 39 refuges are dotted across 23 counties encompassing 26 state legislative districts (see table 1). In July 2004, district senators and representatives were sent an informational newsletter inviting them to the open houses. In addition to these districts, an additional 15 adjoining state districts were contacted and provided the same information, for a total of 42 legislative districts represented by 42 senators and 84 representatives.

Tribal Coordination

On June 10, 2004, six Native American Tribal governments in North and South Dakota (Sisseton-Wahpeton Sioux, Spirit Lake Tribal Council, Standing Rock Sioux, Three Affiliated Tribes, Fort Peck Tribal Executive Board, and the Turtle Mountain Band of Chippewa) were contacted through a letter signed by Service regional director. The letter gave information about the upcoming CCP and invited recipients to serve on the core team. The Service received one inquiry from the Chairman of the Turtle Mountain Band of Chippewas. After receiving clarification on the CCP, the Chairman wished

to continue receiving correspondence, but felt the planning area would not be of interest to his tribal members.

Results of Scoping

Table 2 summarizes all scoping activities. Comments collected from scoping meetings and correspondence, including comment forms, were used in the development of a final list of issues that need to be addressed in the CCP. The planning team determined which alternatives could best address these issues. The preferred alternative formed the basis for the objective and strategies to achieve the goals developed by the planning team. This process ensures that those issues that have the greatest impact on the Program are resolved or given priority over the life of this plan. Identified issues along with some discussion of their impacts to the resource are summarized in chapter 2.

Table 1. North Dakota counties and legislative districts by refuge

County	Population (2002)	Legislative Districts	Refuges in County/District
Barnes	11,224	6	Hobart Lake, Stoney Slough, and Tomahawk NWRs
Benson	6,873	7 and 23	Pleasant Lake, Silver Lake, and Wood Lake NWRs
Bottineau	6,898	6	Lords Lake NWR (also Rolette County)
Burleigh	70,987	8, 14, 30, 32, 35, and 47	Canfield Lake NWR
Dickey	5,554	26 and 28	Dakota Lake and Maple River NWR
Eddy	2,627	23 and 29	Johnson Lake NWR
Emmons	4,087	28	Springwater, Sunburst Lake, and Appert Lake NWRs
Grand Forks	64,929	17, 19, and 43	Little Goose NWR
Grant	2,689	31	Pretty Rock NWR
Griggs	2,599	23	Sibley Lake NWR
Kidder	2,591	14	Hutchinson Lake and Lake George NWRs
Lamoure	4,569	26, 28, and 29	Bone Hill NWR
McHenry	5,739	7	Cottonwood Lake and Wintering River NWRs
McLean	9,014	4 and 8	Camp Lake, Hiddenwood, Lake Otis, and Lost Lake NWRs
Morton	25,181	31, 33, 34, and 36	Lake Patricia NWR
Nelson	3,464	23	Lambs Lake, Rose Lake, and Johnson Lake (Eddy) NWRs
Pierce	4,525	7	Buffalo Lake NWR
Ramsey	11,746	15	Silver Lake NWR (also Benson County)
Rolette	13,760	9	Rabb Lake, School Section Lake, and Willow Lake NWRs
Sheridan	1,572	7 and 14	Sheyenne Lake NWR
Stutsman	21,388	12 and 29	Half Way NWR
Towner	2,712	10 and 15	Brumba, Rock Lake, and Snyder Lake NWRs
Walsh	11,891	16	Ardoch NWR

Source: Office of Social and Economic Trend Analysis 2002; North Dakota Legislative Branch 2006.

Table 2. North Dakota limited-interest refuges planning process summary

Date	Event	Outcome
Dec. 11–12, 2003	Initial meeting with proposed planning team	CCP overview, planning team finalized, purposes identified, initial issues and qualities list, initiate development of mailing list
Feb. 10–11, 2004	Kickoff meeting	Initiate rights discussion, revise issues and qualities list, biological needs identified, plan public scoping
Feb. 19, 2004	Service's rights discussion with regional office leadership	Develop a position paper for the planning team to review on the Service rights on these limited-interest refuges
March 30, 2004	Finalize rights position	Developed a management decision on which rights the Service will control based on the easement agreement and historical records
March–May 2004	Landowners contacted	Landowner newsletter, comment forms
June 1, 2004	Public scoping planning	Open house model developed
June 29, 2004	Public scoping planning	Finalize scoping meeting schedules and formats
July 14, 2004	Maple River open house	Opportunity for public to learn about the CCP and provide comments
July 19, 2004	Bone Hill open house	Opportunity for public to learn about the CCP and provide comments
July 20, 2004	Silver Lake, Wood Lake, Pleasant Lake open house	Opportunity for public to learn about the CCP and provide comments
July 20, 2004	Rose Lake, Lambs Lake, and Little Goose open house	Opportunity for public to learn about the CCP and provide comments
July 20, 2004	Cottonwood Lake, Wintering River and Buffalo Lake open house	Opportunity for public to learn about the CCP and provide comments
July 21, 2004	Hobart Lake, Stoney Slough, and Tomahawk open house	Opportunity for public to learn about the CCP and provide comments
July 21, 2004	Hiddenwood open house	Opportunity for public to learn about the CCP and provide comments
July 22, 2004	Dakota Lake open house	Opportunity for public to learn about the CCP and provide comments
July 22, 2004	Lords Lake, Willow Lake, Rabb Lake, School Section Lake open house	Opportunity for public to learn about the CCP and provide comments
July 27, 2004	Brumba, Snyder Lake, and Rock Lake open house	Opportunity for public to learn about the CCP and provide comments
July 27, 2004	Sheyenne Lake open house	Opportunity for public to learn about the CCP and provide comments
July 27, 2004	Ardoch Lake open house	Opportunity for public to learn about the CCP and provide comments
July 27 and 28, 2004	Appert, Canfield, and Hutchinson Lakes, Lake George, Springwater, Sunburst Lake open house	Opportunity for public to learn about the CCP and provide comments
July 28, 2004	Johnson Lake and Sibley Lake open house	Opportunity for public to learn about the CCP and provide comments
July 29, 2004	Lost Lake open house	Opportunity for public to learn about the CCP and provide comments
Aug. 10, 2004	Halfway Lake meeting	Meet with Half Way Lake landowners, discuss CCP
Aug. 11, 2004	Lake Patricia open house	Opportunity for public to learn about the CCP

Table 2. North Dakota limited-interest refuges planning process summary

Date	Event	Outcome
Sept. 16, 2004	Second Dakota Lake open house	Second opportunity for the public to provide comments about Dakota Lake refuge and the CCP
Dec. 6–7, 2004	Vision, goals, and alternatives workshop	Developed a vision statement, goals, and discussed alternatives for the CCP
Feb. 7–8, 2005	Objectives and strategies workshop	Drafted a set of objectives and strategies for the proposed action
March–April 2005	Prepare draft plan	Planning team prepared first draft of the combined environmental assessment and plan
May 2005	Planning team reviews plan	Planning team reviewed first draft of the CCP and provided comments
July 2005	Internal review of CCP	Service staff from other divisions review draft CCP
August—Sept. 2005	Prepare outreach plan	Conduct outreach with Service partners regarding various issues addressed in the draft CCP
September 23, 2005	Camp Lake landowners meeting	Update the Camp Lake NWR on the progress of the draft CCP to date
October 4, 2005	Publish NOA and release draft plan to the public	Public began reviewing draft CCP
October 12, 2005	Arrowwood District public meetings, Valley City, ND	Present draft CCP and collect public comments
October 18, 2005	Devils Lake (Devils Lake, ND) and Arrowwood District (Henry, ND) public meetings	Present draft CCP and collect public comments
October 25, 2005	Kulm District public meeting, Oakes, ND	Present draft CCP and collect public comments
October 26, 2005	J. Clark Salyer District public meeting, Upham, ND	Present draft CCP and collect public comments
October 27, 2005	Long Lake District public meeting, Moffitt, ND	Present draft CCP and collect public comments
December 2, 2005	Public review ends	All comments are compiled and provided to planning team
December 7, 2005	Planning team reviews public comments	Planning team discussed public comments and recommended changes to the document
December 12, 2005	Brief regional director	Provide a summary of public comments for Directors review
January 2006	Brief Washington Office and edit document	Respond to public comments in the document and make necessary changes. Provide Washington Office a briefing on the public's response to the draft CCP and the Service's response.
April 6, 2006	Final Internal Review Ends	Final one-week internal review for Service staff
April 14, 2006	FONSI signed by regional director	Preferred alternative is selected and became the management direction for the final CCP

Chapter 2. The North Dakota Limited-interest Refuge Program

2.1 Establishment of the Program

In the 1930s, the United States was faced with a depression, a massive drought, and declining waterfowl and other wildlife populations. To address these crises, the federal government developed the Program. Working with states and private landowners, beginning in 1935, dozens of limited-interest refuge agreements were signed. These refuge and flowage easements (see section 2.4 for more information), most perpetual, were established for the purposes of 1) water conservation, 2) drought relief, 3) migratory bird and wildlife conservation purposes.

The economic crisis was also addressed through this Program. The Works Progress/Programs Administration and Civilian Conservation Corps programs provided jobs in the local communities to build the structures needed to impound and control water levels. This reliable water source was not only critical to wildlife but to the livelihood of the landowners and their agricultural operations.

Although most were perpetually protected, a new status was given to these lands in the late 1930s and 1940s. Refuge lands in close proximity were combined, establishing an approved acquisition boundary, and designated as Migratory Bird Sanctuaries (later changed to national wildlife refuges) under the authorities of executive orders and conservation laws. To this day, 93 percent of these lands still remain in private ownership making them unique among the more than 540 national wildlife refuges.

Since this Program was established, it has played a vital role in the recovery and protection of water resources and the waterfowl and other wildlife that depend on these areas. However, these refuges need to be re-evaluated to determine which can truly function as national wildlife refuges as prescribed in the Improvement Act. This should be accomplished through this CCP and future planning efforts.

2.2 Current Status of the Program

The North Dakota Limited-interest National Wildlife Refuges encompass 47,296 limited-interest refuge acres within the boundaries of 39 individual refuges ranging in size from 160 acres (Half Way Lake NWR) to 5,506 acres (Rock Lake NWR). The approved acquisition boundary for these refuges totals 54,140 acres (see figure 2 for locations of these refuges).

Six different managing stations are responsible for this Program including Arrowwood NWR Complex, Audubon NWR Complex, Devils Lake WMD, J. Clark Salyer NWR Complex, Kulm WMD, and Long Lake NWR Complex. Table 3 provides a breakdown of refuges managed by station. Most of these refuges are located east of the Missouri River except for two, Lake Patricia NWR and Pretty Rock NWR. All refuges have an overriding purpose of providing habitat for migratory birds.

No staff or funding is dedicated to this Program. Historically, management has been incidental to the station's other funded programs. Currently no volunteers or Friends Groups assist the Program.

The Limited-interest Refuge Program is not part of the more well-known grassland and wetland easement refuge programs.

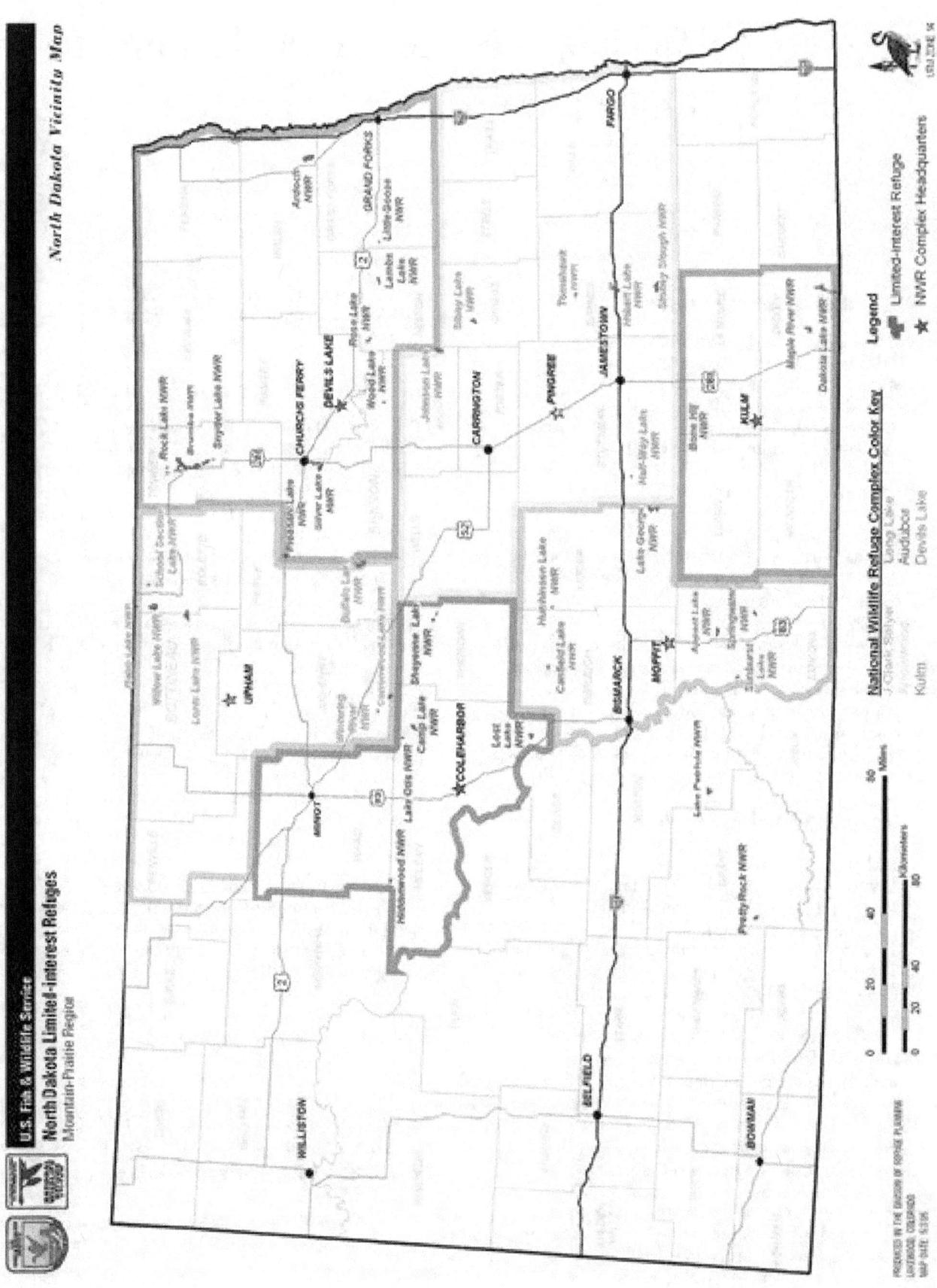

Figure 2. Location Map

Table 3. List of refuges by managing station

Complex Headquarters	Limited-interest Refuge	Limited-interest Refuge Acres	NWR Fee Acres	Total Acres	Approved Acquisition Boundary	WPA Acres	
						Within Approved Acquisition Boundary	Adjacent
Arrowwood NWR Complex 6 Refuges 6,392 Total Limited-interest Refuge Acres 7,445 Approved Acquisition Boundary Acres*	Half Way Lake	160.00	0	160.00	160.00	0	0
	Hobart Lake	1,831.21	245.89	2,077.10	1,840.00	0	0
	Johnson Lake	2,003.42	4.49	2,007.91	1,928.00	0	0
	Sibley Lake	1,077.40	0	1,077.40	1,077.00	81	496
	Stoney Slough	880.00	0	880.00	2,000.00	1,120	440
	Tomahawk	440.00	0	440.00	440.00	0	0
Audubon NWR Complex 7 Refuges 4,831 Total Limited-interest Refuge Acres 6,888 Approved Acquisition Boundary Acres*	Camp Lake	584.70	0	584.70	1,212.44	0	0
	Hiddenwood	568.35	0	568.35	568.00	0	0
	Lake Otis	320.00	0	320.00	640.00	0	0
	Lake Patricia	800.23	0	800.23	1,434.23	0	0
	Lost Lake	960.21	0	960.21	960.00	0	0
	Pretty Rock	800.00	0	800.00	800.00	0	0
	Sheyenne Lake	797.30	0	797.30	1,273.00	0	0
Devils Lake WMD 10 Refuges 18,099 Total Limited-interest Refuge Acres 19,700 Approved Acquisition Boundary Acres*	Ardoch	2,388.50	307.63	2,696.13	2,980.00	0	0
	Brumba	1,977.48	0	1,977.48	1,977.48	0	0
	Lambs Lake	1,026.67	0	1,026.67	1,318.00	80	0
	Little Goose	288.41	0	288.41	359.04	71	0
	Pleasant Lake	897.80	0	897.80	1,020.00	103	0
	Rock Lake	5,505.96	0	5,505.96	5,587.00	0	0
	Rose Lake	836.30	0	836.30	1,280.00	0	134
	Silver Lake	3,347.64	0	3,347.64	3,348.00	0	0
	Snyder Lake	1,550.18	0	1,550.18	1,550.18	0	0
	Wood Lake	280.00	0	280.00	280.00	0	0
J. Clark Salyer NWR Complex 7 Refuges 7,886 Total Limited-interest Refuge Acres 9,221 Approved Acquisition Boundary Acres*	Buffalo Lake	1,539.92	23.80	1,563.72	2,105.00	0	0
	Cottonwood Lake	1,013.47	0	1,013.47	1,013.00	0	0
	Lords Lake	1,915.29	0	1,915.29	1,915.22	0	0
	Rabb Lake	260.80	0	260.80	261.00	0	0
	School Section Lake	297.30	0	297.30	680.00	0	0
	Willow Lake	2,619.69	0.69	2,620.38	2,848.00	227	19
	Wintering River	239.26	0	239.26	399.12	160	106
Kulm WMD 3 Refuges 4,152 Total Limited-interest Refuge Acres 4,544 Approved Acquisition Boundary Acres*	Bone Hill	640.00	0	640.00	640.00	0	0
	Dakota Lake	2,799.78	0	2,799.78	2,784.00	0	0
	Maple River	712.00	0	712.00	1,120.00	408	6

Table 3. List of refuges by managing station

Complex Headquarters	Limited-interest Refuge	Limited-interest Refuge Acres	NWR Fee Acres	Total Acres	Approved Acquisition Boundary	WPA Acres Within Approved Acquisition Boundary	Adjacent
Long Lake NWR Complex 6 Refuges 5,754 Total Limited-interest Refuge Acres 6,343 Approved Acquisition Boundary Acres[1]	Appert Lake	907.75	0	907.75	1,162.76	251	0
	Canfield Lake	310.13	3.10	313.23	453.00	149	631
	Hutchinson Lake	478.90	0	478.90	478.90	0	0
	Lake George	3,089.61	29.20	3,118.81	3,113.00	0	0
	Springwater	640.00	0	640.00	640.00	0	0
	Sunburst Lake	327.51	0	327.51	494.96	178	403

[1]NWR = national wildlife refuge; WPA = Waterfowl Production Area.

Rick Coleman, assistant regional director for refuges, examines a historical 1930s boundary sign found on Buffalo Lake NWR.

2.3 U.S. Fish and Wildlife Service and Landowner Rights

Since the Program was established, some have questioned what rights the government purchased from the landowners relative to the refuges. Overall, the variations in the limited-interest refuge agreements are whether the agreement was perpetual or revocable, and whether it was a flowage and/or limited-interest refuge. Most agreements include the following standard language:

The exclusive (and perpetual) right and easement to flood with water, and to maintain and operate an artificial lake, and/or to raise the water level of a natural lake or stream, upon the land

herein after described, by means of dams, dikes, fills, ditches, spillways, and other structures, for water conservation, drought relief, and for migratory bird and other wildlife conservation purposes, and/or upon said lands and waters to operate and maintain a wildlife conservation demonstration unit and a closed refuge and reservation for migratory birds and other wildlife.

The planning team needed to determine which rights the Service would regulate prior to planning the future of the Program. To make this determination, the planning team examined dozens of historical documents, correspondence, and several solicitor's opinions to better understand the intent of the Program and define such terms as "wildlife conservation demonstration unit" and "closed refuge and reservation for migratory birds."

The limited-interest refuge agreements with a flowage provision focus on the impoundment or main body of water. In the 1930s and 1940s, the federal government funded the installation of dams, dikes, spillways, and other structures to impound and manage water for water conservation and wildlife habitat. The Service also has a senior water right on 38 of the refuges. The Service's water rights to the impoundment or main body of water may be through structures or an established water right, and provide authority to manage water uses. The Service manages water uses, including fishing, boating, and water skiing, to minimize or eliminate negative impacts on migratory birds and other wetland-dependent wildlife.

Hunting, especially market hunting, was an issue at the time the refuges were established. It was clear in the documentation that the Service was given the right to control hunting, including the right to allow it. Trapping was identified as an economic benefit of the limited-interest refuges when the Program was established. Over time, trapping has become more a recreational use than an economic use. Today, trapping has become a management tool necessary to control unnaturally high populations of predators of nesting waterfowl and other grassland birds. The Service issues special use permits to each individual trapper.

According to limited-interest refuge agreements and historical records, it appears the intent was not to control the uses that occur on the uplands or naturally occurring wetlands, apart from hunting. Many of these refuges are farmed, grazed, or have been developed. In some cases, development took place prior to the limited-interest refuge agreements, in particular, farmsteads and recreational cabins.

There is no clearly defined Service right to control activities in uplands, even though the activities may impact upland-dependent wildlife.

Some naturally occurring wetlands have a significant value to wetland-dependent wildlife. However, there appears to be no clearly defined right in the agreements or the historical records that the Service intended to control the management and uses that occur on wetlands.

The planning team developed a final list of rights and uses they felt the Service should and should not regulate based on the authority of the limited-interest refuge agreement and the intent of the Program as described in historical documents:

Uses the Service will regulate include:

- all hunting and trapping activities;
- water level management of impoundments;
- management/regulation of any activities that occur on the impoundments or main body of water to minimize or eliminate

negative impacts on migratory birds and other wetland-dependent wildlife.

Uses the Service will not regulate include:

- any development or other activities (other than hunting) that occur on the uplands;
- management of naturally occurring wetlands.

If the Service wishes to control these uses it will work with willing landowners to provide additional compensation through other programs to acquire these rights (see chapter 6 for more information).

2.4 Purposes of the Limited-interest Refuges

For this plan, the refuges are combined to evaluate them as a group and a Program. The purposes and management capabilities and challenges are similar for all 39 refuges.

All limited-interest refuges were established and are regulated by the associated refuge and/or flowage easements. Where flowage easements were acquired, the Service also filed for water rights using the process established by North Dakota law existing at the time. Even though these lands became national wildlife refuges, the refuge and/or flowage easement language (see previous section) is the overriding purpose on lands that remain in private ownership. The language of the establishing legislation is relevant only to those lands owned by the government. Information, including the refuge purpose, for each of the 39 refuges is summarized in table 4).

Starting in 1939, approved acquisition boundaries were established around adjoining limited-interest refuges and designated as Migratory Bird Sanctuaries, later renamed national wildlife refuges. The overriding purpose of these refuges is management of migratory birds.

Thirty-one refuges established under executive orders signed in 1939 by President F.D. Roosevelt: "as a refuge and breeding ground for migratory birds and other wildlife."

Seven refuges established in 1948 under a precursor to the Fish and Wildlife Coordination Act (August 14, 1946, 60, Stat. 1080): "shall be administered by him [Secretary of Interior] directly or in accordance with cooperative agreements ... and in accordance with such rules and regulations for the conservation, maintenance, and management of wildlife, resources thereof, and its habitat thereon."

In 1971 the limited-interest refuge that covers what is now Lake Otis NWR was "rediscovered" at which time the Director established it as a refuge under the Migratory Bird Conservation Act: "for use as an inviolate sanctuary, or for any other management purpose, for migratory birds."

All goals, objectives, and strategies are intended to support the individual purposes for which each refuge was established.

2.5 Vision and Goals

After public scoping, the Service developed a vision for the Program. A vision describes what will be different in the future as a result of the CCP and the essence of what the Service is trying to do for these refuges and its partners. The vision is a future-oriented statement designed to be achieved through refuge management by the end of the 15-year CCP planning horizon.

Vision Statement

Since our Nation's beginning, great flocks of wildfowl—ducks, geese and water-birds—provided sights and sounds, food and feather. These wings of migration not only inspired hunters but some of our greatest artists, photographers, and poets. In the 1980s, much of the United States, including North Dakota, was gripped by a devastating drought and depression. Hot winds that dried crops also dried wetlands. Wildfowl numbers plummeted, and the skies grew quiet.

Americans took this crisis and saw opportunity and a great partnership was formed. Conservation leaders, the state of North Dakota, the federal government, and private landowners laid the foundation for what would become the North Dakota Limited-interest Program. This Program addressed both wildlife conservation and economic needs. The Works

Progress/Program Administration and Civilian Conservation Corp brought jobs to the communities building dams and other structures to create water areas that now provide habitat and sanctuary for waterfowl and other migratory birds.

Through cooperation with the current refuge landowners and other conservation partners, the Program will realize its full potential. It will become a premier example of private land partnerships promoting fish and wildlife conservation, supporting other conservation programs while continuing to serve as sanctuaries for international migratory birds.

Goals

The Service also developed a set of goals for the Program based on the Improvement Act and information gathered during CCP planning. Five goals were identified.

Goal 1. Wetland Habitat: Maintain and manage natural and created wetlands within the approved acquisition boundary to provide habitat for international populations of waterfowl and other migratory birds along with other wetland-dependent wildlife.

Goal 2. Upland Habitat: Establish a land protection program within the approved acquisition boundary to maintain, restore, and enhance uplands to provide habitat for international populations of waterfowl, other migratory birds, and other wildlife.

Goal 3. Partnerships: Foster beneficial landowner, community, and regional partnerships to assist in achieving the Program vision while ensuring 100 percent of all partners gain a greater understanding of the management and resources of the limited-interest refuges.

Goals 4. Visitor Services: Where compatible, and in cooperation with willing landowners, allow public fishing, hunting, trapping, and other quality wildlife-dependent recreation opportunities that foster an appreciation and understanding of the management and resources of the Program and the System.

Goal 5. Administration: Secure and effectively use funding, staffing, and partnerships to ensure the Program meets its full potential of habitat protection and visitor use.

Table 4. Acres, establishment date, legislation, and purpose(s) for each refuge

Refuge	Limited-interest Refuge Acres	Fee-title Acres	Approved Acquisition Boundary Acres	Establishment Date and Boundary Approval	Establishment Legislation or Executive Order (EO)	Refuge Purpose(s)
Appert Lake	997.75	0	1,162.76	May 10, 1939	EO 8110	"as a refuge and breeding ground for migratory birds and other wildlife."
Ardoch	2,388.50	307.63	2,980.00	June 12, 1939	EO 8147	"as a refuge and breeding ground for migratory birds and other wildlife."
Bone Hill	640.00	0	640.00	May 10, 1939	EO 8162	"as a refuge and breeding ground for migratory birds and other wildlife."
Brumba	1,977.48	0	1,977.48	June 12, 1939	EO 8148	"as a refuge and breeding ground for migratory birds and other wildlife."
Buffalo Lake	1,539.92	28.99	2,105.00	May 10, 1939	EO 8113	"as a refuge and breeding ground for migratory birds and other wildlife."
Camp Lake	584.70	0	1,212.44	May 10, 1939	EO 8114	"as a refuge and breeding ground for migratory birds and other wildlife."
Canfield Lake	310.13	3.10	453.00	May 10, 1939	EO 8115 (limited-interest refuge acres) Migratory Bird Conservation Act (3.10 fee-title acres)	"for use as an inviolate sanctuary, or for any other management purpose, for migratory birds."
Cottonwood Lake	1,013.47	0	1,013.00	June 12, 1939	EO 8149	"as a refuge and breeding ground for migratory birds and other wildlife."
Dakota Lake	2,799.78	0	2,784.00	May 10, 1939	EO 8117	"as a refuge and breeding ground for migratory birds and other wildlife."
Half Way Lake	160.00	0	160.00	May 10, 1939	EO 8120	"as a refuge and breeding ground for migratory birds and other wildlife."
Hiddenwood	568.86	0	568.00	June 12, 1939	EO 8150	"as a refuge and breeding ground for migratory birds and other wildlife."
Hobart Lake	1,881.21	245.89	1,840.00	June 12, 1939	EO 8151	"as a refuge and breeding ground for migratory birds and other wildlife."
Hutchinson Lake	478.90	0	478.90	May 10, 1939	EO 8121	"as a refuge and breeding ground for migratory birds and other wildlife."
Johnson Lake	2,003.42	4.49	1,928.00	May 10, 1939	EO 8120	"as a refuge and breeding ground for migratory birds and other wildlife."
Lake George	3,080.61	29.20	3,113.00	June 12, 1939	EO 8153	"as a refuge and breeding ground for migratory birds and other wildlife."

Table 4. Acres, establishment date, legislation, and purpose(s) for each refuge

Refuge	Limited-interest Refuge Acres	Fee-title Acres	Approved Acquisition Boundary Acres	Establishment Date and Boundary Approval	Establishment Legislation or Executive Order (EO)	Refuge Purpose(s)
Lake Otis	320.00	0	640.00	Aug. 4, 1971	Migratory Bird Conservation Act	"for use as an inviolate sanctuary, or for any other management purpose, for migratory birds."
Lake Patricia	800.28	0	1,434.23	June 12, 1939	EO 8156	"as a refuge and breeding ground for migratory birds and other wildlife."
Lambs Lake	1,206.67	0	1,318.00	June 12, 1939	EO 8159	"as a refuge and breeding ground for migratory birds and other wildlife."
Little Goose	288.41	0	359.04	May 10, 1939	EO 8125	"as a refuge and breeding ground for migratory birds and other wildlife."
Lords Lake	1,915.29	0	1,915.22	May 10, 1939	EO 8127	"as a refuge and breeding ground for migratory birds and other wildlife."
Lost Lake	960.21	0	960.00	May 10, 1939	EO 8128	"as a refuge and breeding ground for migratory birds and other wildlife."
Maple River	712.00	0	1,120.00	June 12, 1939	EO 8162	"as a refuge and breeding ground for migratory birds and other wildlife."
Pleasant Lake	897.80	0	1,020.00	June 12, 1939	EO 8164	"as a refuge and breeding ground for migratory birds and other wildlife."
Pretty Rock	800.00	0	800.00	Feb. 3, 1941	EO 8659	"as a refuge and breeding ground for migratory birds and other wildlife."
Rabb Lake	261.90	0	261.00	Dec. 21, 1948	Act of August 14, 1946 (precursor to the Fish and Wildlife Coordination Act)	"shall be administered ... for the conservation, maintenance, and management of wildlife resources thereof, and its habitat thereon."
Rock Lake	5,505.96	0	5,587.00	June 12, 1939	EO 8165	"as a refuge and breeding ground for migratory birds and other wildlife."
Rose Lake	889.30	0	1,280.00	Dec. 21, 1948	Act of August 14, 1946 (precursor to the Fish and Wildlife Coordination Act)	"shall be administered ... for the conservation, maintenance, and management of wildlife resources thereof, and its habitat thereon."
School Section Lake	297.30	0	680.00	Dec. 21, 1948	Act of August 14, 1946 (precursor to the Fish and Wildlife Coordination Act)	"shall be administered ... for the conservation, maintenance, and management of wildlife resources thereof, and its habitat thereon."

Table 4. Acres, establishment date, legislation, and purposes) for each refuge

Refuge	Limited-interest Refuge Acres	Fee-title Acres	Approved Acquisition Boundary Acres	Establishment Date and Boundary Approval	Establishment Legislation or Executive Order (EO)	Refuge Purpose(s)
Sheyenne Lake	797.90	0	1,273.00	Dec. 21, 1948	Act of August 14, 1946 (precursor to the Fish and Wildlife Coordination Act)	"shall be administered ... for the conservation, maintenance, and management of wildlife resources thereof, and its habitat thereon."
Sibley Lake	1,077.40	0	1,077.00	June 12, 1939	EO 8157	"as a refuge and breeding ground for migratory birds and other wildlife."
Silver Lake	3,347.64	0	3,348.00	Dec. 21, 1948	Act of August 14, 1946 (precursor to the Fish and Wildlife Coordination Act)	"shall be administered ... for the conservation, maintenance, and management of wildlife resources thereof, and its habitat thereon."
Snyder Lake	1,550.18	0	1,550.18	Feb. 3, 1941	EO 8660	"as a refuge and breeding ground for migratory birds and other wildlife."
Springwater	640.00	0	640.00	Feb. 3, 1941	EO 8661	"as a refuge and breeding ground for migratory birds and other wildlife."
Stoney Slough	880.00	0	2,000.00	Feb. 3, 1941	EO 8653	"as a refuge and breeding ground for migratory birds and other wildlife."
Sunburst Lake	327.51	0	494.96	Feb. 3, 1941	EO 8664	"as a refuge and breeding ground for migratory birds and other wildlife."
Tomahawk	440.00	0	440.00	Feb. 3, 1941	EO 8655	"as a refuge and breeding ground for migratory birds and other wildlife."
Willow Lake	2,619.69	0.69	2,848.00	Dec. 21, 1948	Act of August 14, 1946 (precursor to the Fish and Wildlife Coordination Act)	"shall be administered ... for the conservation, maintenance, and management of wildlife resources thereof, and its habitat thereon."
Wintering River	239.26	0	399.12	Feb. 3, 1941	EO 8657	"as a refuge and breeding ground for migratory birds and other wildlife."
Wood Lake	280.00	0	280.00	Dec. 21, 1948	Act of August 14, 1946 (precursor to the Fish and Wildlife Coordination Act)	"shall be administered ... for the conservation, maintenance, and management of wildlife resources thereof, and its habitat thereon."
Totals	**47,296.17**	**614.8**	**54,140.33**			

2.6 Special Values

The planning team and public identified special values and qualities that make most of these refuges valuable for wildlife and the American people. The limited-interest refuges:

- contribute to a complex of habitats;
- complement other conservation lands;
- provide nesting, staging, and resting areas for waterfowl;
- provide habitat for other migratory birds;
- provide a reliable water source for migratory birds during critical migration periods;
- increase hunting opportunities in surrounding areas;
- maintain water quality and quantity;
- have secure senior water rights (38 of 39 refuges);
- provide cultural value
  - historical value of the Program (dustbowl, waterfowl decline)
  - local history (Works Progress/Project Administration and Civilian Conservation Corps projects);
- provide wildlife observation opportunities;
- serve as wildlife sanctuaries.

Yellowlegs
Bob Hines/USFWS

2.7 Issues

A final list of issues was developed following an analysis of all comments collected from refuge staffs, public scoping activities, and a review of the requirements of the Improvement Act and NEPA. Substantive comments (i.e., those that could be addressed within the authority of the limited-interest refuge agreement and the management capabilities of the Service) were considered during the formulation of the alternatives for future management. Major issues are summarized below.

Wetland Management

The Service acquired the rights to "flood with water, and to maintain and operate an artificial lake, and/or to raise the water level of a natural lake or stream, upon the land ... for water conservation, drought relief, and for migratory bird and wildlife conservation purposes." The Service also was granted the right to install structures necessary to achieve this purpose. Most of the work began in the 1930s through the Works Progress/Program Administration and Civilian Conservation Corps. Since that time, no funding or staffing has been committed for management and maintenance of created wetlands and structures. Structures have been replaced as funds become available; however, most structures are original and are in disrepair, or do not meet the standards necessary to effectively manage water for wildlife purposes.

In addition, the Service has not had funding or staffing to manage naturally occurring wetlands, currently estimated at nearly 3,000 acres. This is a significant resource for a variety of wildlife species, in particular waterfowl, shorebirds, and wading birds. If the Service wishes to protect wetlands, it must work with willing landowners to determine adequate compensation for this added protection (see section 6.3).

Upland Management

The Service regulates hunting and trapping in uplands. Development, farming, and grazing existed and have expanded on many of the limited-interest refuges since this Program was initiated 70 years ago. In some cases, these activities have caused a complete loss of biodiversity and wildlife habitat. Most refuges have varying intensities of impacts including the loss of wetlands and native grasslands.

According to "Habitat and Population Evaluation Team" (HAPET) data, about 14,060 acres of native prairie occurs on the limited-interest refuges. Most of this acreage is used for grazing and haying; however, farming and development patterns change and once this prairie is broken for farming or construction, it will be lost forever. The continued loss of upland habitat, in particular native prairie, will have the greatest impact to wildlife and the future of the Program.

Partnerships

Over 225 landowners own 93 percent of the lands within the boundaries of the limited-interest refuges. Some landowners' parents or other relatives signed the easement refuge agreements and current landowners have since inherited the properties. In some cases, landowners were unaware the easement refuge existed. There has never been an avenue or program that has allowed for consistent, quality dialogue between landowners and the Service. Some efforts have been made to work with landowners when maintenance or rehabilitation of structures has been completed, but overall there has been little contact. Several landowners prefer this lack of contact, while others wish to be more informed on management plans and opportunities to receive compensation for additional protections such as wetland and grassland easement refuges or fee title. Assistance has occasionally been requested for maintaining water level management structures.

The Program will not succeed without the partnership of these landowners. While some of the limited-interest refuges have remained unchanged over the life of the limited-interest refuge, others have been developed extensively. Many landowners would like assistance or compensation for managing their uplands for wildlife. However, except for a few acquisitions including some additional limited-interest refuges, no funding or staffing have been allocated for this Program since it was initiated.

Some partners have shown interest in providing assistance in maintaining these refuges; however, because most limited-interest refuges are on private lands, few incentives exist for national organizations to assist in maintenance and rehabilitation. The Service's Private Lands Program has been successful in North Dakota; however, because the limited-interest refuges already have some

protection, few attempts have been made to use this program's limited resources for the limited-interest refuges. Most of the work accomplished on the limited-interest refuges, including boundary posting, structure maintenance, and law enforcement, is incidental to the managing stations' other funded programs.

Visitor Services

The Improvement Act recognized that wildlife-dependent recreational uses involving hunting, fishing, wildlife observation and photography, and environmental education and interpretation, when determined to be compatible, are legitimate and appropriate public uses of the Refuge System. However, even if a use is found to be compatible on a refuge, it may not be permitted unless the resources are available to manage that use.

The NDGF was particularly interested in determining the landowner's willingness and compatibility of opening as many refuges as possible to provide increased recreational opportunities.

No public use on any limited-interest refuge will be permitted without access being granted by willing landowners. The Service has never had the right to permit access to the public without the landowners' permission.

In addition, the Service cannot open refuges to any uses unless they are open to the general public. Restrictions may be placed on the number of users through permits and drawings; however, no restrictions can be placed on who may participate. The following summarizes the issues related to wildlife-dependent programs.

Consumptive Uses (hunting, fishing, and trapping). The Service has the right to control all hunting, trapping, and fishing within the boundaries of the limited-interest refuges. This includes the right to allow these uses when found compatible with the purposes and funding and staffing are available to manage the program.

Hunting and Trapping. Hunting and trapping are considered by many, including the Service, to be a legitimate, traditional recreational use of renewable natural resources. National wildlife refuges exist primarily to safeguard wildlife populations through habitat preservation. The word "refuge" includes the idea of providing a haven of safety for wildlife and, as such, hunting and trapping might seem an inconsistent use of the System. However, habitat that typically supports healthy wildlife populations produces harvestable surpluses that are a renewable resource.

A number of landowners commented about crop and landscaping damage due to the concentration of white-tailed deer and geese. In particular, during hunting seasons, wildlife concentrate in protected areas and impact crops and landscaping due to this unnatural concentration of animals and lack of food. There is no concern that these wildlife species are in peril or declining in number. The populations are at harvestable levels.

When historical records were examined, increased trapping opportunities was seen as a benefit to establishing these refuges. At that time this benefit was more economic than biological. Since established, trapping has been permitted on these refuges on a permit-only basis. The use today is minimal, less than one trapper per refuge. However, this trapping program has become vital to the success of nesting waterfowl and grassland birds, the purpose for which these refuges were established. Studies indicate that the major source of mortality for waterfowl during the breeding season is predation (Sargeant and Reveling 1992), with greater than 70% of nest failures attributed to predation (Sovada et. al. 2001). The predator community of the prairie pothole region has drastically changed as habitat was modified by agriculture. The resulting highly cultivated and heavily fragmented landscape is more conducive to smaller predators such as fox, raccoon and skunk than it is for wolves and grizzlies. Smaller predators now occur at very high densities across the prairie breeding grounds. These smaller predators prey heavily on all ground nesting birds, including ducks. The result is that we now rarely observe nesting success in ducks over 15%, which is likely the break even point for most populations of waterfowl. This is a human-caused problem and without intervention, these small predator bases would continue to expand and devastate waterfowl and other ground nesting bird populations.

Fishing. Fishing is currently permitted on only a few refuges. The Service does control this use but must receive permission for public access from the landowners. Although the Service controls fishing, it looks to the state to assist in managing those areas open to fishing. The state currently stocks several lakes open to the public with game fish. The landowners, the state, and the managing stations requested that we examine additional opportunities for fishing on other refuges in this project area. There was particular interest in ice fishing, a popular sport throughout the state. The Service will ensure that any current or proposed uses are compatible with the purposes of each refuge.

Boy Fishing
Paul Kerris/USFWS

Nonconsumptive Uses (wildlife observation and photography, environmental education and interpretation). Wildlife-dependent nonconsumptive uses such as wildlife observation, photography, environmental education, and interpretation, are priority public uses of the System. None of these activities are currently promoted on the limited-interest refuges. Public access must be granted by the landowners and the use must be found compatible before any public uses are permitted. It is not known what opportunities exist for these uses. However, there was some interest at public meetings and from a few landowners to develop trails and provide environmental education and interpretation opportunities, in particular for students.

Administration

Since it was established almost 70 years ago, only cursory attempts have been made to provide the guidance and resources necessary to properly manage the Program. Overall, this

Program is managed and funded incidental to the managing stations' other funded programs, such as management of fee-title refuge lands and WPAs. Funding and staffing are already insufficient to manage the current fee-title and limited-interest refuge land bases. The managing stations spend an average of only 5 days per year working on the limited-interest refuges, partly as a result of limited management abilities afforded by the limited-interest refuge agreement. However, the lack of attention has equated to a loss of biodiversity and management capability as areas become developed and water management structures lose integrity.

Divestiture

The North Dakota Limited-interest Program was initiated to address a variety of issues relevant in the 1930s including a widespread depression and drought, market hunting, and wildlife preservation. This was also the era of one of the largest land conservation movements in history. Many of the national wildlife refuges in existence today were established during this era by such conservation leaders as J. Clark Salyer, Jr., Ding Darling, and Director M.O. Steen. This was also the time President Franklin Roosevelt introduced the "New Deal," which created such programs as the Works Progress/Project Administration and the Civilian Conservation Corps.

Representatives from the Bureau of Biological Survey (precursor the U.S. Fish and Wildlife Service) traveled throughout North Dakota and other states meeting with landowners and securing refuge and/or flowage easements. Hundreds of these easements were signed followed by dozens of limited-interest refuges being established through executive order and other legislation. Local communities were provided jobs as water management structures were built to provide critical water for migratory birds and livestock.

In the 1950s, there was an effort to re-evaluate each refuge to determine its ability to function as a refuge. A field team from the Service traveled to each refuge and habitats were evaluated at a cursory level. Many refuges were heavily impacted by development, while some easement agreements had been acquired on areas that possessed little or no wildlife habitat. Although the process is not well documented, it appears that dozens of limited-interest refuges were divested based on this report.

Following this effort, several limited-interest refuges began to receive greater attention. Some of them have since become fully functioning national wildlife refuges, primarily due to land acquisitions.

The most recent divestiture of a limited-interest refuge occurred in 1999 on Lake Elsie National Wildlife Refuge. Public Law 105-312, adopted October 30, 1998 (110 Stat. 2957), terminated the Service's easement on 634.7 acres and repealed Executive Order 8152, thus abolishing the refuge. The Service requested the action, as all migratory bird values had been lost to development, which under the terms of the easement and EO creating the refuge, the Service had no authority to control. This same justification is being used for several of the limited-interest refuges proposed for divestiture in this document.

This CCP process is only the second recorded attempt to comprehensively evaluate the limited-interest refuges and determine each refuge's worthiness to be part of the System. It is critical to complete this evaluation. Any resources obtained for this Program must be used on those refuges that truly have the potential to meet the purposes for which they were established and the goals and mission of the System. Refuges that cannot meet this standard, or that have been or can be managed by the state of North Dakota, which owns many of these refuge lands, must be considered for divestiture.

Chapter 3. Alternatives

3.1 Introduction

Alternatives are different approaches designed to achieve the refuge purpose(s), vision, and the goals identified in the CCP while helping to fulfill the System's mission.

This chapter describes the two alternatives analyzed in detail for the Program, including alternative A (current management—no action) and alternative B (enhance the program). The following sections describe how the alternatives were developed and how they addressed the substantive issues identified during the scoping process.

This CCP and EA have been completed at the programmatic level, rather than as a management plan for each refuge. This was the most logical approach given the following circumstances:

- 39 limited-interest refuges in the CCP
- Private ownership of 93 percent of the limited-interest refuge lands
- Similarity of purposes, limited-interest refuge agreement language, and management history
- All but two are located east of the Missouri River, scattered from the Canadian to South Dakota borders
- No established guidelines or resources to manage the refuges or the Program

3.2 Alternatives Development

In 2004, the Service held several meetings with the landowners, public, and agencies to identify issues and concerns associated with the establishment and management of the Program. The public involvement process is summarized in greater detail in chapter 2. Based on public input, as well as guidance from the Improvement Act, NEPA, and Service planning policy, the planning team selected six substantive issues to be addressed in the alternatives:

1. Wetland Management
2. Upland Management
3. Partnerships
4. Visitor Services
5. Administration
6. Divestiture

A more detailed description of each issue is in section 2.7.

Once the decision was made to prepare a programmatic plan, it was discussed how to develop alternatives for meeting the goals while addressing these substantive issues. Given the circumstances mentioned previously, in particular, the fact that there were no current management guidelines, it was felt that the only alternative other than no action was to "enhance the program."

Any proposed actions beyond the uses the Service will regulate (see section 2.3) will not be conducted without the full support of the affected landowners.

3.3 Alternatives Considered but Eliminated from Detailed Study

When the planning process began and the issues for these refuges and the program were identified, the planning team recognized that there was a great deal of similarity in purposes, habitats, issues, and limited management capabilities (see section 2.3) for all of 39 refuges. Given these facts, there was no added value in developing individual goals, objectives, and strategies for each refuge.

3.4 Elements Common to All Alternatives

This section identifies key elements included in the CCP regardless of which alternative was selected. Both alternatives would incorporate the following:

- No alternative would infringe on any landowner rights or commercial uses, beyond the uses the Service would regulate under the authority of the limited-interest refuge agreement (as described in section 2.3), without permission from willing landowners.
- Landowners would have the right to refuse receiving any additional compensation for added protections.
- Activities outside the authority of the limited-interest refuge agreement would not be conducted unless permission is granted from affected, willing landowners.
- Landowners would be provided with information on the Program annually.
- The Service would minimize negative impacts to migratory birds and other wildlife by regulating uses that occur on water.
- The Service would ensure that refuge management complies with all other federal laws and regulations that provide direction for managing units of the System.

Chapter 6 outlines the Service's plan for implementing the Enhancing the Program alternative in the form of goals, objectives, and strategies.

3.5 Description of Alternatives

The theme and general management direction for each alternative are described below.

Alternative A—Current Management (No Action)

Alternative A, the no-action alternative, describes current and future management of the Program. It provides the baseline against which to compare the preferred alternative. It is also a requirement of NEPA that the no-action alternative be addressed.

General Management Direction

Management would continue to be incidental to other refuge programs. Visitor services would see few changes due to a lack of funding and staffing to manage additional uses.

Upland and wetland habitat, in particular native prairie, would continue to be lost and landowners would not receive any further compensation for habitat protections. Water management structures would continue to deteriorate. Any repairs to water management structures would be funded through the maintenance and management program.

Current hunting and trapping programs would continue if they are determined to be compatible with the refuge purposes. Only a few refuges are open to hunting while each refuge has been opened to permit-only trapping since they were established. The trapping program is limited, less than one trapper per refuge; however, this program is vital to increasing ground nesting bird survival by reducing unnaturally high populations of small predators (including raccoons and skunks). This permit-only trapping would continue.

Contact with landowners and other partners would be incidental to issues and common interests.

No limited-interest refuges would be divested, further straining limited resources and affecting the integrity of the System due to the retention of refuges that do not support the mission or goals of the System.

Activities outside the authority of the limited-interest refuge agreement would not be conducted unless permission is granted from willing landowners.

Alternative B—Preferred Alternative (Enhance the Program)

Alternative B, the preferred alternative, would address these refuges and their identified issues at a programmatic level while assisting the refuges to reach their full potential though greater cooperation and support.

General Management Direction

Highest priority would be given to ensuring that landowners become true partners in this Program and are involved in future management. A full-time Program manager would be recruited to oversee the Program and implement this CCP. Landowners would be contacted at least annually through an informational newsletter providing updates on Program changes, opportunities, and limited-interest refuge news. Partnerships with state agencies and other organizations would be actively pursued to achieve common goals that may support and enhance the Program.

Using available habitat data, each managing station would work with the Habitat and Population Evaluation Team to develop a protection priority list for each refuge. Native prairie habitat would be given highest priority as areas are ranked, followed by natural wetlands. This would be the first critical evaluation of the value of each refuge and would assist managers in prioritizing the use of limited funding and staffing.

With assistance from the Regional Engineering Office, existing impoundments would be evaluated to determine needed repairs or replacement of water management structures such as spillways, dams, and water control structures. Following evaluation, repairs, or replacement, impoundments would be managed for wetland-dependent migratory birds under the guidelines of an established water level management plan.

Existing public use programs would continue if they remain compatible and there is a continued demand. Trapping would continue on a permit-only basis focusing efforts on maximizing waterfowl and other grassland nesting bird success through predator control. Public ice fishing would be permitted, where compatible.

The Service would work with willing landowners to determine their interest in providing access to the public for additional hunting, fishing, wildlife observation and photography, environmental education and interpretation programs. As new opportunities arise, each manager would determine the compatibility of such activities based on the refuge purposes and available resources to manage the proposed use. All programs must be made available to the public, but no public uses will occur unless the landowners grant access. Even though these refuges are primarily on private lands, any public programs are governed under the Code of Federal Regulations; therefore, public participation may not be restricted beyond such restrictions as limiting the number of users and seasons.

Under this alternative, six refuges would be proposed for divestiture: Camp Lake, Lake Patricia, Sheyenne Lake, School Section Lake, Bone Hill, and Cottonwood Lake. These refuges are being considered for divestiture due to extensive loss of habitat and ownership patterns. In particular, the state currently owns and/or manages three of these refuges (Lake Patricia, Sheyenne Lake, and School Section Lake) and are willing to continue if they are divested. The state has also expressed an interest in the fisheries resources of the remaining three refuges although these refuges uplands have little value to wildlife due to extensive development and commercial operations. The Service does not control these upland uses under the limited-interest refuge agreement; therefore, the uses have expanded over the 70 years. These proposals would ensure that future resources are expended on the remaining refuges that still have the potential to support the mission and goals of the System.

In all cases, activities outside the authority of the limited-interest refuge agreement would not be conducted unless permission is granted from the affected and willing landowners including, but not limited to:

- additional compensation for added protections of wildlife habitat;
- fee-title acquisitions;
- visitor services programs where access is needed from the landowner.

3.6 Comparison of Alternatives

The two alternatives evaluated are no action and enhance the program (the preferred alternative). A comparison of these alternatives is shown in table 5.

Blue-winged Teal
Tom Kelley/USFWS

Table 5. Summary comparison of alternatives

Focus Area	Alternative A (Current Management—No Action)	Alternative B (Enhance the North Dakota Limited-interest Program)
Wetland Management	Retain current structures acquiring funds from the Maintenance Management System program for incidental repair/rehab Little to no water level management of existing impoundments No management or protection of natural wetlands. No actions would be conducted beyond the authority of the current limited-interest refuge agreement (see section 2.3).	Evaluate existing structures, prioritize projects and repair or replace as needed to meet modern water level management standards while not exceeding current water right levels. Actively manage those impoundments with the ability to support migratory birds, particularly waterfowl. Work with willing landowners to protect and enhance naturally occurring wetlands. Monitor wildlife response to management actions. No actions would be conducted beyond the authority of the current limited-interest refuge agreement (see section 2.3) without the permission of willing landowners. Work with willing landowners to restore and enhance riparian habitats.
Upland Management	No management of upland habitat or uses. No actions would be conducted beyond the authority of the current limited-interest refuge agreement (see section 2.3).	Managing stations will work with the HAPET office to prioritize refuges and upland habitat types for added protections, giving priority to native habitats. Provide assistance and compensation to willing landowners for added protections of upland habitat. Monitor wildlife response to management actions. Provide farmers with information through the Department of Agriculture on best management practices to reduce siltation and contaminants. No actions would be conducted beyond the authority of the current limited-interest refuge agreement (see section 2.3) without the permission of willing landowners.

Table 5. Summary comparison of alternatives

Focus Area	Alternative A (Current Management—No Action)	Alternative B (Enhance the North Dakota Limited-interest Program)
Partnerships	Annually update landowner mailing list. Contact with landowners and other partners would be incidental to issues and common interests.	Same as alternative A except: Prepare an annual newsletter for the landowners and other interested partners providing information on the Program including compensated programs available to willing landowners and include a postage-paid comment form to provide feedback to the Service. Provide opportunities for landowners to record wildlife sightings on their properties. Highlight sightings in annual newsletters. Notify landowners when management actions have the potential to affect their lands. Work with NDGF to collaborate on refuge evaluations for habitat protection and visitor services programs. Actively develop partnerships to work on common interests that may benefit the Program.
Visitor Services		
Hunting, Trapping, and Fishing	No new hunting or fishing opportunities would be permitted unless compatible with the refuge purposes, resources are available, and landowners provide access. No waterfowl (ducks) hunting would be permitted. Trapping would continue on a permit-only basis focusing all efforts on improving nesting success of waterfowl and other ground nesting birds through a predator management program. Trappers will follow state regulations and annually report species harvested.	Same as alternative A, except: Managing stations would actively work with willing landowners and the NDGF to evaluate each refuge for hunting and fishing opportunities. Depredation issues would be addressed through these programs. Four seasonal law enforcement officers would be recruited to ensure the safety of visitors, landowners, and wildlife. Ice fishing would be permitted, where appropriate and compatible.
Wildlife Observation and Photography	No active watchable wildlife programs.	Managing stations would actively work with landowners to determine their willingness to provide wildlife viewing opportunities. Develop wildlife observation programs.
Environmental Education	No environmental education programs.	Managing stations would actively work with landowners to determine their willingness to provide environmental education opportunities. Work with the Service's Visitor Services Division and local teachers to develop environmental education programs highlighting the Program and its resources.

Table 5. Summary comparison of alternatives

Focus Area	Alternative A (Current Management—No Action)	Alternative B (Enhance the North Dakota Limited-interest Program)
Administration	No dedicated resources would be available for the Program.	Recruit one statewide Program manager. Develop Maintenance Management System projects to repair or replace water management structures. Develop project proposals for compensating willing landowners for added protections.
Divestiture	No refuges would be divested.	Six refuges would be divested due to habitat loss and opportunities for state management. Future resources available for the Program would be used on those refuges that have the ability and qualities needed to support the goals of the National Wildlife Refuge System.

Chapter 4. Affected Environment

4.1 Physical Environment

The limited-interest refuges are scattered across North Dakota, primarily east of the Missouri River, from the Canadian border down to South Dakota. Because the refuges cover such a large geographic area, the physical environment and biological resources will be described in terms of the physiographic region or ecoregion in which each refuge or group of refuges is located. Thirteen ecoregions are found in the Program area (figure 5). These ecoregions denote areas of general similarity in ecosystems and the type, quality, and quantity of environmental resources.

The text and graphics in this section are from a project completed in 1998 by the Northern Prairie Wildlife Research Center in Jamestown, North Dakota and titled "Ecoregions of North and South Dakota."

Ecological regions are distinguished by the patterns of biotic and abiotic phenomena that reflect the differences in ecosystem quality. These phenomena include geology, physiography, vegetation, climate, soils, land use, wildlife, and hydrology. Each ecoregion and its associated refuge(s) are summarized in tables 6 and 7.

Glacial Lake Agassiz Basin

From the Pembina Escarpment, the view of the Glacial Lake Agassiz Basin (figure 3) is of an extremely flat patchwork of cultivated farmland. Because the Red River of the North has a poorly defined flood plain and very low gradient, flooding can be a problem. Outside of channelized areas in the flood plain, turbid valley streams meander within narrow buffer strips of cottonwood, elm, ash, and willow. Soils range from silty to clayey in texture. Most areas have high water tables and are extremely productive.

Refuge: Ardoch NWR (also Saline Area)

Figure 3. Glacial Lake Agassiz Basin Ecoregion

Missouri Plateau

On the Missouri Plateau west of the Missouri River (figure 4), the landscape opens up to become the "wide open spaces" of the American West. The topography of this ecoregion was largely unaffected by glaciation and retains its original soils and complex stream drainage pattern. A mosaic of spring wheat, alfalfa, and grazing land covers the shortgrass prairie where herds of bison, pronghorn (antelope), and elk once grazed.

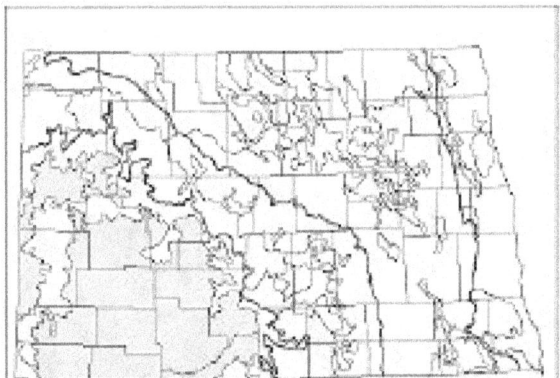

Refuges: Lake Patricia and Pretty Rock NWRs

Figure 4. Missouri Plateau Ecoregion

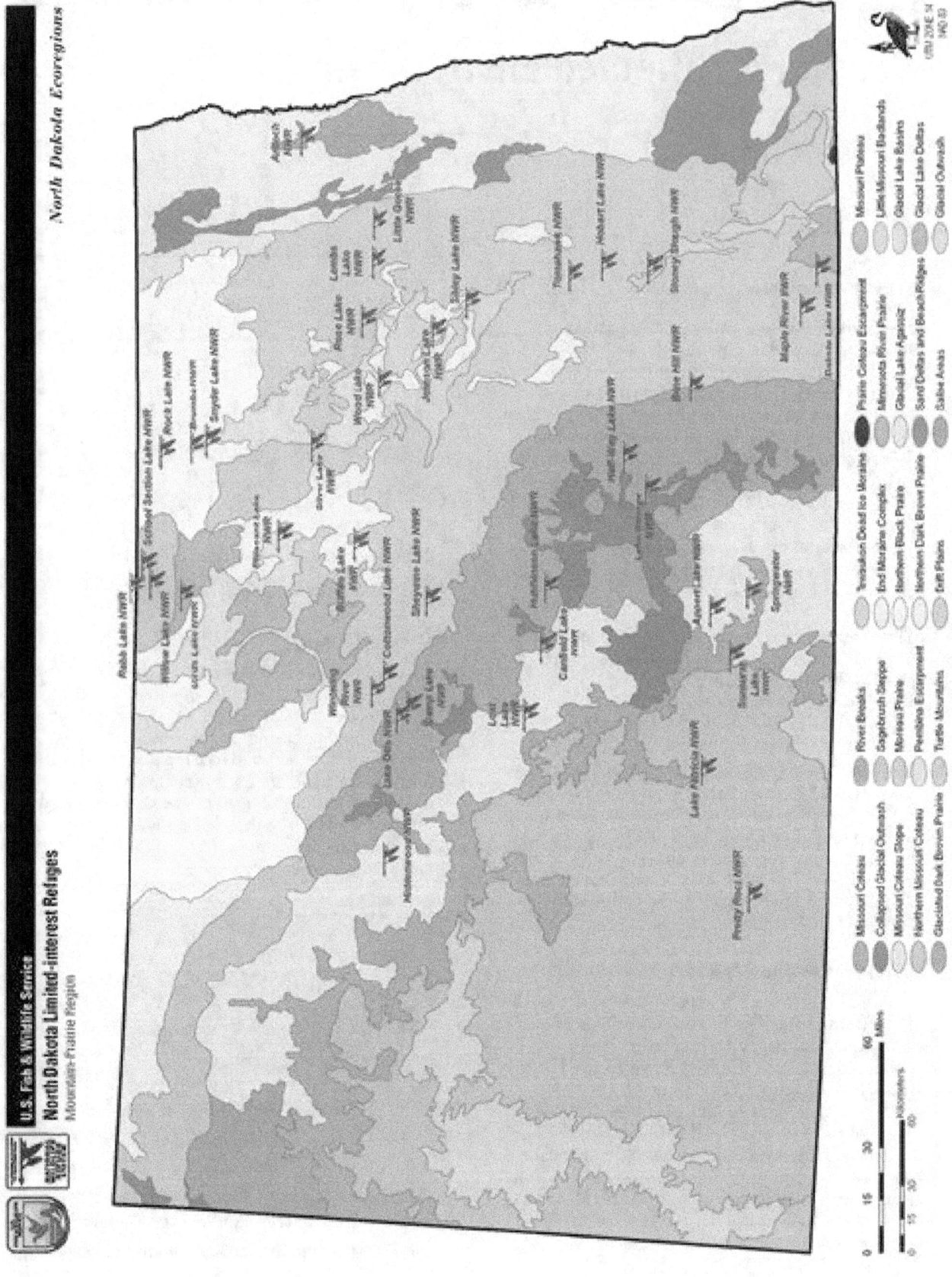

Figure 5. Ecoregion Map

River Breaks

The River Breaks (figure 6) form broken terraces and uplands that descend to the Missouri River and its major tributaries. These terraces have formed particularly in soft, easily erodible strata, such as Pierre shale. The dissected topography, wooded draws, and uncultivated areas provide a haven for wildlife. Riparian gallery forests of cottonwood and green ash persist along major tributaries such as the Moreau and Cheyenne rivers, but have largely been eliminated along the Missouri River by impoundments.

Refuges: Sunburst Lake and Springwater NWRs

Figure 6. River Breaks Ecoregion

Drift Plains

On the Drift Plains (figure 7), the retreating Wisconsinan glaciers left a subtle undulating topography and a thick mantle of glacial till. A greater proportion of temporary and seasonal wetlands are found on the Drift Plains than in the Coteau areas, where semipermanent wetlands are numerous. Because of the productive soil and level topography, this ecoregion is almost entirely cultivated, with many wetlands drained or simply tilled and planted. However, valuable waterfowl habitat still remains, concentrated in state and federally sponsored duck production areas. The historic grassland on the Drift Plains was a transitional mix of tallgrass and shortgrass prairie. The prairie grasses have been largely replaced by fields of spring wheat, barley, sunflowers, and alfalfa.

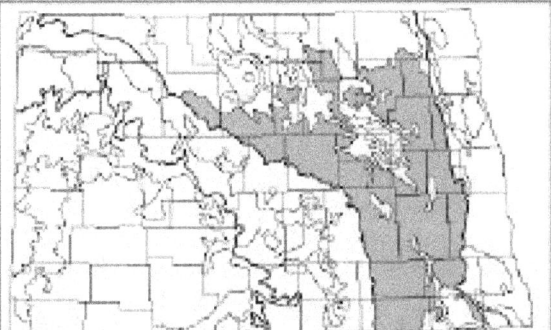

Refuges: Bone Hill (also Missouri Coteau), Buffalo Lake (also End Moraine Complex), Dakota Lake (also Glacial Lake Delta), Maple River, Hobart Lake, Tomahawk, Rose Lake, Lambs Lake, Little Goose, Wintering River, Cottonwood Lake, Sheyenne Lake, and Stoney Slough NWRs (also Glacial Outwash)

Figure 7. Drift Plains Ecoregion

End Moraine Complex

The End Moraine Complex (figure 8) is a concentration of glacial features in east central North Dakota. Blue Mountain and Devils Lake Mountain are composed of blocks of surficial material scraped off and thrust up by the continental glacier at the south end of the Devils Lake basin. In the western part of the ecoregion, patches of stagnation moraine similar to the Missouri Coteau have high wetland densities. On the moraines south of Devils Lake basin, favorable precipitation, aspect, and slightly higher elevations result in wooded lake margins and morainal ridges.

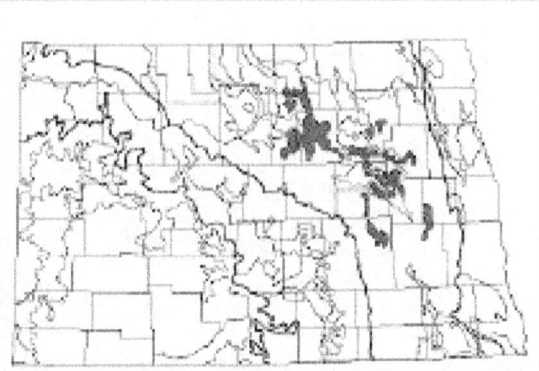

Refuges: Buffalo Lake (also Drift Plains), Johnson Lake (also Glacial Outwash), and Wood Lake NWRs

Figure 8. End Moraine Complex Ecoregion

Glacial Lake Basins

The Glacial Lake Basins (figure 9) were once occupied by Lake Souris, Devils Lake, and Lake Dakota. These proglacial lakes were formed when major stream or river drainages were blocked by glacial ice during the Pleistocene. The smooth topography of the Glacial Lake Basins, even flatter than the surrounding Drift Plains, resulted from the slow buildup of water-laid sediments. The level, deep soils on the lake plains are intensively cultivated. In the north, the primary crops are spring wheat, other small grains, and sunflowers; in the Lake Dakota basin of South Dakota, corn and soybeans are more prevalent.

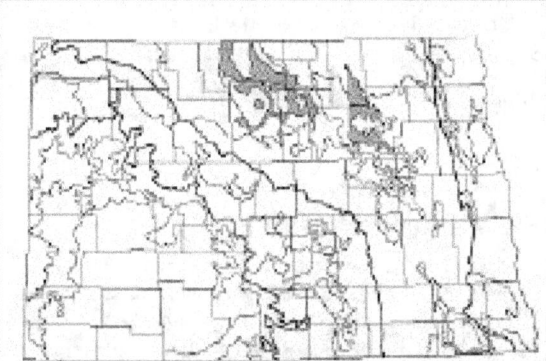

Refuges: Pleasant Lake, Dakota Lake (also Drift Plains), Silver Lake, Rock Lake and Brumba (both also in Northern Black Prairie), and Snyder Lake NWRs

Figure 9. Glacial Lake Basins Ecoregion

Glacial Outwash

The disjunct areas of Glacial Outwash (figure 10) differ from outwash areas on the Missouri Coteau in that they generally have a smoother topography. The soils are highly permeable with low water holding capacity. Areas of excessive soil permeability have a poor to fair potential for dryland crop production. Some areas are used for irrigated agriculture. The risk for blowing soil in droughty areas is reduced by retaining native range grasses like little bluestem, needle-and-thread grass, and green needlegrass.

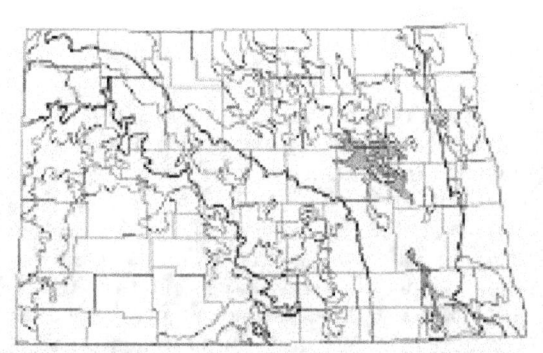

Refuges: Sibley Lake, Johnson Lake (also End Moraine Complex), and Stoney Slough NWRs (also Drift Plains)

Figure 10. Glacial Outwash Ecoregion

Northern Black Prairie

The Northern Black Prairie (figure 11) represents a broad phenological transition zone marking the introduction from the north of a boreal influence in climate. Aspen and birch appear in wooded areas, willows grow on wetland perimeters, and rough fescue, common to the Rocky Mountain foothills, becomes evident in grassland associations. This ecoregion has the shortest growing season and the lowest January temperatures of any other ecoregion in the Dakotas. Most of the area is used for growing small grains, with durum wheat being a major crop.

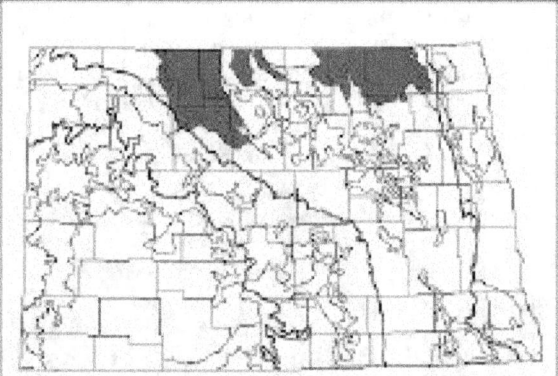

Refuges: Rock Lake and Brumba NWRs (both also in Glacial Lake Basins)

Figure 11. Northern Black Prairie Ecoregion

Turtle Mountains

The undulating landscape and abundant wetlands of the Turtle Mountains (figure 12) are similar to the Missouri Coteau. However, the Turtle Mountains contain larger, deeper, and more numerous lakes. Additionally, this ecoregion receives about 10 inches more precipitation than the surrounding Drift Plains; thus, it supports a forest cover of aspen, birch, burr oak, elm, and ash. The forest soils are erodible and poorly suited for cropland, though there is some clearing for pastureland.

Refuges: Rabb Lake, Willow Lake, and School Section Lake NWRs

Figure 12. Turtle Mountains Ecoregion

Missouri Coteau

Like closely spaced ocean swells, the rolling hummocks of the Missouri Coteau (figure 13) enclose countless wetland depressions or potholes. During its slow retreat, the Wisconsinan glacier stalled on the Missouri escarpment for thousands of years, melting slowly beneath a mantle of sediment to create the characteristic pothole topography of the Coteau. The wetlands of the Missouri Coteau and the neighboring prairie pothole regions are the major WPAs in North America. Land use on the Coteau is a mix of tilled agriculture in flatter areas and grazing land on steeper slopes.

Refuges: Half Way Lake, Lake George, Hutchinson Lake, Canfield Lake, Camp Lake, Lake Otis, and Bone Hill NWRs (also Drift Plains)

Figure 13. Missouri Coteau Ecoregion

Missouri Coteau Slope

The Missouri Coteau Slope ecoregion (figure 14) declines in elevation from the Missouri Coteau to the Missouri River. Unlike the Missouri Coteau where there is a paucity of streams, the Missouri Coteau Slope has a simple drainage pattern and fewer wetland depressions. Due to the level to gently rolling topography, there is more cropland than on the Missouri Coteau. Cattle graze on the steeper land that occurs along drainages.

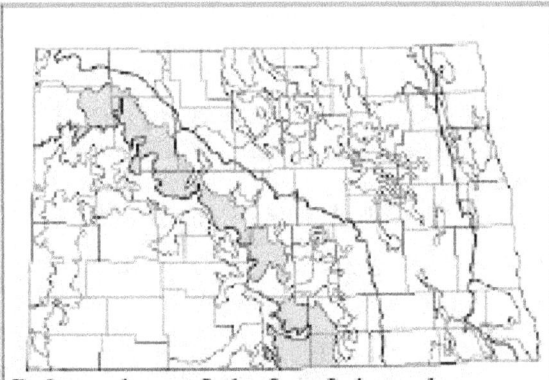

Refuges: Appert Lake, Lost Lake, and Hiddenwood NWRs

Figure 14. Missouri Coteau Slope Ecoregion

Glacial Lake Deltas

The Glacial Lake Deltas (figure 15) were deposited by rivers entering glacial lake basins (e.g., Glacial Lake Souris, Devils Lake, and Lake Dakota). The heaviest sediments, mostly sand and fine gravel, formed delta fans at the river inlets. As the lake floors were exposed during withdrawal of the glacial ice, wind reworked the sand in some areas into dunes. In contrast to the highly productive, intensively tilled glacial lake plains, the dunes in the delta areas have a thin vegetative cover and a high risk for wind erosion. These areas are used mainly for grazing or irrigated agriculture.

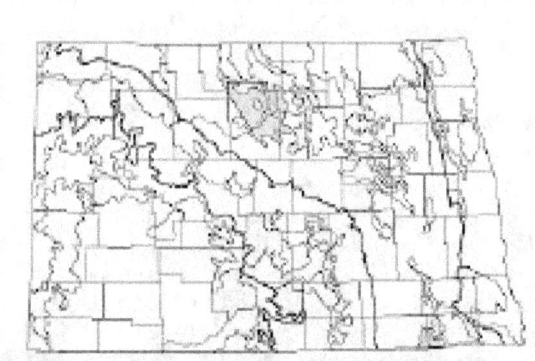

Refuges: Dakota Lake (also Drift Plains and Glacial Lake Basins), and Lords Lake NWRs

Figure 15. Glacial Lake Deltas Ecoregion

Saline Area

In the Saline Area (figure 16) of the Lake Agassiz basin, salty artesian groundwater flows to the surface through glacial till and lacustrine sediments from the underlying beds of Cretaceous sandstone. The regional boundary of the Saline Area delineates an area where salt effects are most evident. Other saline areas occur along the tributaries of the Park, Forest, and Turtle rivers in northeast North Dakota. Salt-affected soils in the saline area reduce crop productivity. Many areas are not suitable for farming, but are used for range or wildlife habitat.

Refuge: Ardoch NWR (also Glacial Lake Agassiz Basin)

Figure 16. Saline Area Ecoregion

Collapsed Glacial Outwash

Areas of Collapsed Glacial Outwash (figure 17) formed from gravel and sand deposited by glacial meltwater and precipitation runoff over stagnant ice. Many large, shallow lakes are found in these areas; lakes and wetlands tend to be slightly to very alkaline depending upon the flowpath of groundwater moving through the permeable outwash deposits. They attract birds preferring large areas of open water, such as white pelicans, black terns, and Forster's terns, as well as those living in brackish water, such as avocets and tundra swans.

Refuge: Lake George NWR (also Missouri Coteau)

Figure 17. Collapsed Glacial Outwash Ecoregion

Table 6. Physiography of the ecoregions in which the limited-interest refuges reside

Ecoregion	Area (miles)	Elevation/Local Relief (feet)	Geology	Soil Order (Great Groups)	Common Soil Series	Potential Natural Vegetation	Land Use and Land Cover	Limited-interest Refuges in Ecoregion
Glacial Lake Agassiz Basin	5,187	790–1,200/1–50 Extremely flat glacial lake plain. Streams and rivers sluggish, meandering, and highly turbid with large sediment loads. Ditching and channelization common.	Tertiary sandstone, shale and some coal. Ludlow, Cannonball, Slope, Bullion Creek, and Sentinel Butte Formations.	Mollisols (Haploborolls, Calciborolls, Argiborolls, Natriborolls)	Vebar, Chama, Amor, Williams, Rhoades, Belfield, Cabba, Flasher, Reeder, Regent, Parshall, Golva, Zahl	Blue grama, wheatgrass/ needlegrass association, little bluestem, prairie sandreed	Dryland farming and cattle grazing. Spring wheat a predominant crop with acreage of barley, oats, and sunflowers, native areas consist of mixed grasses.	Ardoch NWR (also Saline)
Missouri Plateau	20,000	1,750–3,300/50–500 Unglaciated. Moderately dissected level to rolling plains with isolated sandstone buttes.	Same as above	Entisols (Ustorthents, Ustipsamments)	Same as above	Same as above	Same as above	Lake Patricia and Pretty Rock NWRs
River Breaks	10,517	1,300–2,700/200–500 Unglaciated. Highly dissected. Highly dissected hills and uplands bordering major rivers and associated alluvial plains.	Tertiary sandstone and shale.	Mollisols (Calciborolls, Haploborolls) Entisols (Ustorthents, Ustipsamments, Ustifluvents) Plaraquents) Aridisols (Natrargids) Vertisols (Haplusterts) Inceptisols (Ustochrepts)	Sansarc, Opal, Bullock, Cabba, Amor, Flasher, Vebar, Tenvik, Mandan, Cherry, Chama, Zahl, Lallie, McKeen	Blue grama, western wheatgrass, buffalograss, and some bluestem. Juniper and deciduous trees on north-facing slopes. Cottonwood gallery forests on the flood plain	Steep slopes restrict land use to cattle grazing. Land cover is mostly rangeland and native grasses. Remnant woodlands in draws and on existing alluvial flats.	Sunburst Lake (also Missouri Coteau Slope) and Springwater NWRs

Table 6. Physiography of the ecoregions in which the limited-interest refuges reside

Ecoregion	Area (mile²)	Elevation/Local Relief (feet)	Geology	Soil Order (Great Groups)	Common Soil Series	Potential Natural Vegetation	Land Use and Land Cover	Limited-interest Refuges in Ecoregion
Drift Plains	15,699	1,080–2,000/0–200. Glaciated. Generally flat, with occasional "washboard" undulations. High concentrations of temporary and seasonal wetlands. Simple drainage pattern.	Glacial till over Cretaceous Pierre Shale and Fox Hills Formations	Mollisols (Haploborolls, Calcisquolls, Natriborolls, Calciborolls, Argiaquolls)	Barnes, Svea, Buse, Hamerly, Cresbard, Parnell	Western wheatgrass, big and little bluestem, switchgrass, and indiangrass	Extensively tilled to spring wheat and other small grains, sunflowers, and alfalfa	Bone Hill (also Missouri Coteau), Dakota Lake (also Glacial Lake Delta and Basins), Hobart Lake, Tomahawk, Silver Lake (also Glacial Lake Basins), Rose Lake, Lambs Lake, Little Goose, Stoney Slough (also Glacial Outwash), Cottonwood Lake, Sheyenne Lake, Maple River, Buffalo Lake (also End Moraine Complex) and Wintering River NWRs
End Moraine Complex	1,518	1,450–1,700/3–170. Glaciated. A diverse area of hummocky stagnation moraine, parallel end moraine ridges, and other glacial features such as eskers, kames and thrust ridges.	Wisconsin glacial till and outwash	Mollisols (Haploborolls, Argiborolls, Calciborolls, Calciaquolls)	Hemdal, Emrick, Esmond, Barnes, Buse, Bottineau, Aastad, Edgeley, Hamerly	Tallgrass/Midgrass prairie; western wheatgrass, green needlegrass, big and bluestem, blue grama. Forest vegetation of bur oak and aspen associated with Devils Lake.	Mixed range and cropland depending up slope and presence of rocks in soil. Spring wheat, oats, barley, flax, and hay.	Buffalo Lake NWR (and Drift Plains) Johnson Lake NWR (also Glacial Outwash) Wood Lake NWR

Table 6. Physiography of the ecoregions in which the limited-interest refuges reside

Ecoregion	Area (mile²)	Elevation/ Local Relief (feet)	Geology	Soil Order (Great Groups)	Common Soil Series	Potential Natural Vegetation	Land Use and Land Cover	Limited-interest Refuges in Ecoregion
Glacial Lake Basins	3,584	1,300–1,585/0–30 Glaciated. Very level glacial lake floors. Low wetland density.	Glacial lake deposits	Mollisols (Calciaquolls, Endoaquolls, Haploborolls, Natriborolls)	Hegne, Fargo, Bearden, Overly, Embden, Gardena, Glyndon, Great Bend, Aberdeen	Western wheatgrass, needle-and-thread grass, blue grama, green needlegrass	Extensively tilled for durum and spring wheat, sunflowers, and flax. Corn and soybeans south.	Pleasant Lake, Dakota Lake (also Drift Plains and Glacial Lake Deltas), Silver Lake (also Drift Plains), Rock Lake and Brumba (both also in Northern Black Prairie), and Snyder Lake NWRs
Glacial Outwash	800	1,300–1,550/0–50 Glaciated. Flat to slightly rolling. Ancient channel depressions, relict lakes.	Sand and plane-bedded gravel, sediments of glacial meltwater rivers	Mollisols (Haploborolls, Natraquolls) Entisols (Udipsamments)	Brantford, Claire, Totten, Renshaw, Arvilla, Fordville, Sioux	Little bluestem, needle-and-thread grass, blue grama, prairie junegrass. Elm, ash, bur oak in river bottoms.	Cattle grazing on droughtiest soils. Tillable land produces wheat, oats, barley, rye, and alfalfa.	Johnson Lake (also End Moraine Complex), Stoney Slough (also Drift Plains) and Sibley Lake NWRs
Northern Black Prairie	5,000	1,500–1,970/5–200 Glaciated. Generally flat, with occasional "washboard" undulations. High concentrations of temporary and seasonal wetlands. Simple drainage pattern.	Glacial till over Cretaceous Pierre Shale and Tertiary Ft. Union Formation.	Mollisols (Haploborolls, Natriborolls, Calciaquolls, Calciborolls, Argiaquolls)	Barnes, Svea, Cresbard, Hamerly, Buse, Parnell	Northern prairie: western wheatgrass, green needlegrass, little bluestem, blue grama, and rough fescue.	Extensively tilled to durum and spring wheat, other small grains, sunflowers and alfalfa	Rock Lake and Brumba Lake NWRs (both also in Glacial Lake Basins)

Table 6. Physiography of the ecoregions in which the limited-interest refuges reside

Ecoregion	Area (mile²)	Elevation/Local Relief (feet)	Geology	Soil Order (Great Groups)	Common Soil Series	Potential Natural Vegetation	Land Use and Land Cover	Limited-interest Refuges in Ecoregion
Turtle Mountains	409	2,000–2,550/40–150. Glaciated. Platform of hummocky, rolling terrain above surrounding drift plains. Stream network lacking. High concentration of large lakes and wetlands.	Glacial till over Tertiary sandstone and shale.	Mollisols (Haploborolls, Argiborolls, Calciborolls) Alfisols (Eutroboralfs)	Bottineau, Buse, Kelvin, Metigoshe	Bur oak dominant on side slopes, aspen on top. Other species present: green ash, paper birch, boxelder, sumac, serviceberry, and snowberry.	Native woodland and pasture clearings. Some hay and small grains on gentler soils.	Rabb Lake, Willow Lake, and School Section Lake NWRs
Missouri Coteau	9,122	1,650–2,100/10–300. Glaciated. Hummocky, rolling stagnation moraine. Stream drainage absent or uncommon. Numerous pothole wetlands between mounds of glacial till.	Thick glacial till over Tertiary sandstone and shale.	Mollisols (Haploborolls, Argiaquolls, Argiborolls, Calciborolls)	Barnes, Buse, Parnell, Svea, Williams, Bowbells, Zahl	Western wheatgrass, bluestem, needle-and-thread grass, green needlegrass Prairie cordgrass, northern reedgrass near wetlands.	Cattle grazing on steeper land mixed with tilled agriculture of hay and spring wheat. Native prairie remaining on unbroken rangeland. Wetlands provide wildlife habitat.	Half Way Lake, Lake George (also Collapsed Glacial Outwash), Bone Hill (also Drift Plains), Hutchinson Lake, Camp Lake, Canfield Lake, and Lake Otis NWRs
Missouri Coteau Slope	5,799	1,700–2,450/50–150. Glaciated. Level to gently rolling plain sloping to Missouri River. Sparse drainage pattern, few wetlands.	Wisconsin glacial till over Tertiary sandstone and shale in Cretaceous Pierre Shale.	Mollisols (Haploborolls, Argiborolls, Argiaquolls, Calciborolls)	Williams, Max, Zahl, Bowbells, Parnell	Western wheatgrass, needle-and-thread grass, prairie junegrass, green needlegrass.	Mainly tilled agriculture of spring wheat, barley, alfalfa, silage corn. Some grazing on steep and saline or wet areas.	Appert Lake, Sunburst Lake (also River Breaks), Lost Lake, and Hiddenwood NWRs

Table 6. Physiography of the ecoregions in which the limited-interest refuges reside

Ecoregion	Area (miles)	Elevation/ Local Relief (feet)	Geology	Soil Order (Great Groups)	Common Soil Series	Potential Natural Vegetation	Land Use and Land Cover	Limited-interest Refuges in Ecoregion
Glacial Lake Delta	1,877	1,290–1,966–85. Glaciated. Flat sheets of sand and gravel or rolling sand dunes. Paucity of stream channels.	Sand and gravel deposited over glacial lake floor	Mollisols (Haploborolls, Calciaquolls, Endoaquolls) Entisols (Udipsamments, Psammaquents)	Heda, Ulen, Arvilla, Sioux, Serden, Rosewood, Lohnes, Bantry, Hamar	Prairie sandreed, little bluestem, indiangrass, switchgrass, sand bluestem	Droughty soils mostly used for native pasture. When tilled, used for small grains, flax and fall planted rye (north) or small grains, sunflowers, and corn (south).	Dakota Lake (also Glacial Lake Basins and Drift Plains) and Lords Lake NWRs
Saline Area	348	830–870/3–25. Glacial Lake plain with saline ground water welling to the surface.	Silt and clay lacustrine deposits over Cretaceous shale and sandstone	Mollisols (Calciaquolls)	Bearden, Antler, Ojata	Tallgrass prairie, salt tolerant western wheatgrass, saltgrass	Grazing land on strongly saline soils. Where salinity levels are moderate, sunflowers, barley, sugarbeets, and potatoes are grown. Brackish wetland habitat	Ardoch NWR (also Glacial Lake Agassiz Basin)
Collapsed Glacial Outwash	1,771	1,650–2,100/30/130. Glaciated. Irregular plains left by glacial outwash deposited over stagnant ice. Broad, shallow, brackish wetlands and lakes.	Late Wisconsin glacial outwash deposits over Tertiary sandstone and shale and Cretaceous Pierre Shale.	Mollisols (Natraquolls, Haploborolls, Calciaquolls, Haplaquolls, Argiaquolls)	Paso, Bowdle, Lehr, Wabek, Telfer, Lihen, Sioux, Parshall, Arvilla, Southam, Divide, Harriet	Needlethread, plains muhly, prairie muhly, prairie junegrass, blue grama. Saltgrass in alkaline areas.	Small grains, sunflowers, alfalfa, and corn on deeper soils. Grazing land on shallow soils over gravel. Sand and gravel quarries. Wetlands provide wildlife habitat.	Lake George NWR (also Missouri Coteau)

Source: Bryce et al. 1998.

Table 7. Climate of the ecoregions in which the limited-interest refuges reside

Ecoregion	Area (miles²)	Temperature/ Moisture Regimes	Precipitation	Frost-Free Mean Annual (days)	Mean Temperature January and July min/max (°F)	Limited-interest Refuges in Ecoregion
Glacial Lake Agassiz Basin	5,197	Frigid/Ustic	15–17	95–130	-3/21;55;88	Ardoch NWR (also Saline)
Missouri Plateau	20,000	Frigid/Ustic	15–17	95–130	-3/21;55;88	Lake Patricia and Pretty Rock NWRs
River Breaks	10,517	Frigid/Ustic	16–18	90–125	-3/21;56;87	Sunburst Lake (also Missouri Coteau Slope) and Springwater NWRs
Drift Plains	15,609	Frigid/Udic	17–19	95–125	-5/16;56;88	Bone Hill (also Missouri Coteau), Dakota Lake (also Glacial Lake Delta and Basins), Hobart Lake, Tomahawk, Silver Lake (also Glacial Lake Basins), Rose Lake, Lambs Lake, Little Goose, Stoney Slough (also Glacial Outwash), Cottonwood Lake, Sheyenne Lake, Maple River, Buffalo Lake (also End Moraine Complex) and Wintering River NWRs
End Moraine Complex	1,518	Frigid/Udic	18–20	90–120	-7/13;55;82	Buffalo Lake NWR (and Drift Plains) Johnson Lake NWR (also Glacial Outwash) Wood Lake NWRs
Glacial Lake Basins	3,584	Frigid/Udic	16–19	95–120	-10/10;54;80	Pleasant Lake, Dakota Lake (also Drift Plains and Glacial Lake Deltas), Silver Lake (also Drift Plains), Rock Lake and Brumba (both also in Northern Black Prairie), and Snyder Lake NWRs
Glacial Outwash	890	Frigid/Udic	16–18	110–130	-6/14;55;81	Johnson Lake (also End Moraine Complex), Stoney Slough (also Drift Plains) and Sibley Lake NWRs
Northern Black Prairie	5,040	Frigid/Udic	16–20	95–120	-10/10;54;80	Rock Lake and Brumba Lake NWRs (both also in Glacial Lake Basins)
Turtle Mountains	409	Frdig/Udic	16–22	95–120	-10/10;53;80	Rabb Lake, Willow Lake, and Schol Section Lake NWRs

Table 7. Climate of the ecoregions in which the limited-interest refuges reside

Ecoregion	Area (miles²)	Temperature/ Moisture Regimes	Precipitation	Frost-Free Mean Annual (days)	Mean Temperature January and July min/max (°F)	Limited-interest Refuges in Ecoregion
Missouri Coteau	9,122	Frigid/Udic, Ustic	15–19	110–130	-9/16,57/81	Half Way Lake, Lake George (also Collapsed Glacial Outwash), Bone Hill (also Drift Plains), Hutchinson Lake, Camp Lake, Canfield Lake, and Lake Otis NWRs
Missouri Coteau Slope	5,799	Frigid/Ustic	15–18	110–130	-2/20,59/86	Appert Lake, Sunburst Lake (also River Breaks), Lost Lake, and Hiddenwood NWRs
Glacial Lake Delta	1,877	Frigid/Udic	16–19 (north) 19–21 (south)	95–120 (north) 120–140 (south)	-10/10,54/80 (north) 4/19,58/85 (south)	Dakota Lake (also Glacial Lake Basins and Drift Plains) and Lords Lake NWRs
Saline Area	948	Frigid/Udic	18–21	95–125	-7/21,59/82	Ardoch NWR (also Glacial Lake Agassiz Basin)
Collapsed Glacial Outwash	1,771	Frigid/Udic, Ustic	15–19	115–130	-2/20,59/86	Lake George NWR (also Missouri Coteau)

Source: Bryce et al. 1998.

Most of the limited-interest refuges have had some form of development or use varying from livestock yards to dozens of recreational cabins (table 8). Currently, 189 landowners reside on these 39 refuges (149 reside on Camp Lake NWR).

Several of the refuges have become popular recreational areas. Many of the refuges had some residential development at the time the limited-interest refuges were acquired, primarily in the form of farmsteads; however, development now includes commercial operations such as a fertilizer plant, recreational facilities, and an elk farm. The limited-interest refuges are scattered across North Dakota, primarily east of the Missouri River, from the Canadian border down to South Dakota.

Travel from the managing station ranges from 15 minutes to two hours. This travel time is relative to the station's ability to conduct regular maintenance and management programs.

4.2 Biological Resources

Most limited-interest refuges are located east of the Missouri River in the area commonly known the "Prairie Pothole Region." The two major categories of habitat types addressed in this CCP are upland (table 9) and wetland (table 10). The only available data relative to these refuges is from the HAPET office in partnership with Ducks Unlimited and the National Wetlands Inventory. To map upland habitat types, the HAPET office used Landsat Thematic Mapper Satellite Imagery (30 meter resolution) using a combination of unsupervised and supervised classification techniques. Image acquisition dates range from May 1992 to September 1996. Thematic Mapper scenes were processed individually and mosaiced to produce a state-wide coverage. The resulting classes of upland habitat are summarized in table 9.

Five separate upland habitat types were mapped using the image classification process: grass/hay/undisturbed, cropland, forest, riparian, and urban. Most uplands within the refuges are classified as cropland, totaling 14,296 acres. The grass/hay/undisturbed habitat type totals 14,069 acres and is used primarily for haying and grazing operations. These areas have the potential to be preserved as native prairie habitat because there is no indication this ground has ever been plowed or

broken. Forested lands total 814 acres, while riparian areas total 96 acres for all refuges. Some refuges encompass sections of small communities, resulting in an urban classification that totals 218 acres.

Currently, the Service only regulates hunting and trapping uses on the 29,483 acres of uplands (see section 2.3).

Wetland mapping was acquired from the National Wetlands Inventory database and interpreted by the HAPET office. Wetland habitat types within the limited-interest refuges include: impoundments; seasonal, temporary, and semi-permanent wetlands; riverine; and lakes. The Service has a water right on each refuge except Lake Otis. Table 11 summarizes those water rights filed with the state of North Dakota.

The main body of water within the limited-interest refuges was a major focus of the agreement, both from a wildlife preservation and water conservation perspective. Dozens of structures were built in the 1930s to impound and control water. Existing waterbodies, such as lakes and rivers, also were covered by this flowage limited-interest refuge and water right. The Service will regulate the uses that occur on these waters (see section 2.3).

Most of the wetland habitat types within the limited-interest refuges are classified as lakes, totaling 12,867 acres. Impoundment habitat accounts for 8,850 acres, encompassing many other wetland habitat acres due to the characteristics of the impoundment habitats. Impoundment habitats vary from deepwater lakes to seasonal, temporary wetlands. Riverine habitat is limited, totaling 176 acres. These three habitat types are areas in which the Service has the right to control uses and manage for wildlife. Naturally occurring wetland habitats including semi-permanent, temporary, and seasonal wetlands, total 2,436 acres. Information for wetlands on all refuges is provided in table 10. The Service does not control the uses and alterations of any of these naturally occurring wetlands not encumbered by a Service easement. Regulatory authority rests with the U.S. Army Corps of Engineers and the U.S. Environmental Protection Agency. As described in section 2.3, it appears from historical documentation that there was never any intent to regulate wetland uses even though these areas are critical habitat to wetland-dependent wildlife.

Most of the limited-interest refuges (30 of 39) have some sort of structure intended to either impound water or allow manipulation of that water for wildlife or flood control. Few of these structures have been updated since they were originally installed in the 1930s and 1940s. Some are in disrepair, while others are functioning but do not meet the standards for modern water level management practices used to enhance wildlife habitat production.

Table 8. Limited-interest refuge agreements and landowner uses and developments

Refuge	No. of Limited-interest Refuge Agreements	Total Limited-interest Refuge Acres	Travel Time from Managing Station (minutes)	Landowners Residing on Limited-interest Refuge Lands	Landowner Uses and/or Developments
Appert Lake	7	908	20	0	Farming
Ardoch	4	2,389	75	1	3 farmsteads (2 abandoned) and outbuildings
Bone Hill	3	640	90	2	2 residences, fertilizer plant, elk farm
Brumba	12	1,978	65	3	3 farmsteads, farming
Buffalo Lake	7	1,540	80	0	1 recreational cabin
Camp Lake	8	585	60	149	238 cabins, boat docks, beach, livestock, and farming
Canfield Lake	4	310	60	0	Cattle grazing
Cottonwood Lake	7	1,014	80	5	2 farmsteads, 3 residences, 1 mobile trailer, 2 boat docks
Dakota Lake	20	2,800	60	1	2 residences, 1 cabin, boat dock and ramp
Half Way Lake	1	160	90	0	Farming and cattle grazing
Hiddenwood	6	568	80	0	Boat dock and ramp, storage, ball diamond, picnic shelter
Hobart Lake	7	1,831	15	3	3 farmsteads, livestock yard
Hutchinson Lake	2	479	60	0	Cattle grazing
Johnson Lake	7	2,003	60	0	Livestock yard and hay land
Lake George	8	3,090	40	1	1 residence, cattle grazing
Lake Otis	1	320	60	0	Livestock
Lake Patricia	5	800	120	0	Farming, recreation, wildlife habitat (state)
Lambs Lake	11	1,207	60	0	2 abandoned residences, livestock yard
Little Goose	3	288	70	0	None
Lords Lake	10	1,915	45	2	2 farmsteads

Table 8. Limited-interest refuge agreements and landowner uses and developments

Refuge	No. of Limited-interest Refuge Agreements	Total Limited-interest Refuge Acres	Travel Time from Managing Station (minutes)	Landowners Residing on Limited-interest Refuge Lands	Landowner Uses and/or Developments
Lost Lake	5	960	50	0	Cattle grazing
Maple River	4	712	45	0	Cattle grazing and farming
Pleasant Lake	4	898	50	1	1 farmstead, livestock yard
Pretty Rock	2	800	180	1	1 farmstead and livestock yard
Rabb Lake	2	261	65	0	None
Rock Lake	37	5,506	70	3	3 farmsteads, farming and cattle grazing
Rose Lake	2	836	20	1	1 farmstead
School Section Lake	3	297	65	1	1 farmstead, cattle grazing
Sheyenne Lake	7	797	60	0	1 boat dock and ramp, recreation, wildlife habitat (state)
Sibley Lake	9	1,077	60	1	1 farmstead, livestock yard
Silver Lake	17	3,348	50	5	7 farmsteads (2 abandoned), livestock yard and farming
Snyder Lake	6	1,550	60	1	Boat ramp
Springwater	2	640	40	0	Cattle grazing
Stoney Slough	9	880	30	1	1 farmstead, organic farm, cattle grazing, recreation
Sunburst Lake	1	328	60	1	1 farmstead, cattle grazing
Tomahawk	4	440	20	2	2 farmsteads, livestock yard
Willow Lake	17	2,620	60	3	3 farmsteads, farming, cattle grazing
Wintering River	2	239	80	0	Abandoned farmstead
Wood Lake	3	280	25	1	1 farmstead, cattle grazing, farming
Totals/Averages	269	47,294	Average = 58	189	

Table 9. Upland habitat types

Refuge	Upland Habitat Types (acres)					Total Upland Acres
	Grass/Hay/ Undisturbed	Cropland	Forest	Riparian	Urban	
Appert Lake	79.53	742.45	0.00	0.00	0.00	821.98
Ardoch	322.11	945.86	26.47	0.00	0.00	1,294.44
Bone Hill	167.87	405.33	0.00	0.00	0.00	573.20
Brumba	606.18	996.59	19.45	0.00	0.00	1,622.22
Buffalo Lake	719.91	167.34	35.45	33.89	0.00	956.58
Camp Lake	286.62	34.20	0.00	0.00	0.00	320.82
Canfield Lake	89.05	0.23	0.00	1.83	0.00	91.10
Cottonwood Lake	421.01	311.62	0.00	0.00	0.00	732.63
Dakota Lake	555.88	922.60	16.98	18.85	0.00	1,514.30
Half Way Lake	40.96	0.51	0.00	0.00	0.00	41.47
Hiddenwood	91.42	469.79	0.00	0.00	0.00	561.22
Hobart Lake	366.51	505.21	2.22	0.00	0.00	873.51
Hutchinson Lake	91.67	1.43	0.00	8.95	0.00	102.06
Johnson Lake	1,032.49	101.08	2.45	0.00	5.74	1,141.76
Lake George	1,330.75	83.07	0.00	18.52	15.35	1,447.68
Lake Otis	307.87	0.10	0.00	0.00	0.00	307.97
Lake Patricia	N.D.*	N.D.	N.D.	N.D.	N.D.	N.D.
Lambs Lake	75.73	2.87	0.18	0.00	0.00	78.78
Little Goose	39.63	278.40	0.00	0.00	0.00	318.03
Lords Lake	553.15	529.05	21.00	0.00	0.00	1,103.20
Lost Lake	611.77	0.23	0.00	0.00	0.00	612.02
Maple River	166.39	563.78	0.00	0.00	0.00	730.17
Pleasant Lake	433.56	18.56	97.81	0.00	20.94	570.86
Pretty Rock	N.D.	N.D.	N.D.	N.D.	N.D.	N.D.
Rabb Lake	18.05	0.34	93.68	0.00	0.00	113.63
Rock Lake	1,312.80	2,953.16	30.94	3.29	53.07	4,353.26
Rose Lake	175.65	553.86	0.00	0.00	0.00	729.51
School Section Lake	26.91	5.23	11.00	0.00	0.00	43.14
Sheyenne Lake	187.68	7.48	0.55	7.31	9.12	212.13
Sibley Lake	481.67	16.97	6.01	0.00	0.00	504.64
Silver Lake	559.11	2,061.64	4.00	0.00	113.59	2,738.34
Snyder Lake	664.80	564.22	0.89	0.00	0.00	1,229.91
Springwater	569.26	44.20	6.23	0.00	0.00	619.70
Stoney Slough	114.22	609.76	0.00	0.00	0.00	723.98
Sunburst Lake	321.53	103.97	0.00	2.89	0.00	428.40
Tomahawk	271.76	76.26	0.00	0.00	0.00	348.02
Willow Lake	740.12	69.93	424.81	0.00	0.00	1,234.86
Wintering River	87.76	76.96	3.43	0.00	0.00	168.15
Wood Lake	138.26	71.30	10.41	0.00	0.00	219.97
Total Acres	14,059.66	14,296.61	813.95	95.48	217.81	29,482.51

*N.D. = No landcover data available.

Source: Service 1998.

Table 10. Wetland habitat types

Refuge	Impoundments (acres)	Wetlands (acres)					NWI Total (acres)	Water Management Structure(s)
		Seasonal	Temporary	Semi-permanent	Riverine (acres)	Lake (acres)		
Appert Lake	71.91	7.48	3.17	72.27	0.00	0.00	82.28	Earthen levee
Ardoch	1,091.00	23.4	12.55	0.79	9.43	1,143.16	1,189.33	Steel screw gate, 2 spillways
Bone Hill	15.03	15.87	0.32	9.12	0.00	43.15	68.95	Earthen dam
Brumba	0.22	57.11	17.02	15.94	13.15	97.73	200.94	2 spillways (earthen and sheet pile)
Buffalo Lake	535.65	16.40	7.66	16.60	3.08	588.96	582.72	Earthen dam, culvert, masonry spillway
Camp Lake	157.86	2.54	0.62	21.04	0.00	143.45	167.56	Earth and rubble dike, concrete spillway, inoperable WCS
Canfield Lake	0.00	11.98	0.00	0.00	0.00	204.38	216.25	None
Cottonwood Lake	0.00	35.92	7.68	16.87	4.98	232.08	297.48	Ditch, concrete culvert
Dakota Lake	549.65	48.98	90.76	64.55	13.16	822.15	1,080.59	Earthen/sheet pile dam with stop log
Half Way Lake	0.00	0.38	0.00	0.19	0.00	116.31	117.41	None
Hiddenwood	0.00	1.50	7.52	0.00	0.00	121.71	190.72	Culvert
Hobart Lake	63.88	4.34	10.14	9.24	0.00	849.79	873.51	None
Hutchinson Lake	0.00	1.74	14.33	36.78	0.00	290.94	343.38	None
Johnson Lake	0.00	1.48	0.67	1.39	0.00	454.80	458.48	Earthen dam and spillway
Lake George	0.00	28.68	30.64	76.55	0.00	1,441.51	1,577.37	2 Earthen dikes, metal spillway
Lake Otis	0.00	12.29	0.11	0.00	0.00	6.29	18.60	None
Lake Patricia	316.83	0.00	0.00	0.00	0.00	339.86	339.83	Earthen dike, WCS, and spillway
Lambs Lake	111.76	30.81	23.40	97.48	0.00	132.47	281.16	Earthen dam and concrete spillway
Little Goose	31.56	0.39	1.11	0.00	0.00	38.90	40.30	Earthen dam and spillway, field crossing
Lords Lake	0.00	32.35	5.45	82.04	0.00	669.50	789.33	2 ditches and 2 earthen dams
Lost Lake	0.00	10.49	10.26	145.73	18.91	163.04	350.42	Dike, diversion ditch, and nesting island, concrete spillway, WCS
Maple River	0.00	19.30	4.01	32.92	35.09	0.00	82.31	Earthen dam and sheet pile weir
Pleasant Lake	0.00	7.69	0.00	11.91	0.00	471.98	491.58	Fence and masonry water control structure
Pretty Rock	183.13	30.51	0.00	0.00	0.00	181.88	212.34	Dike and WCS

Table 10. Wetland habitat types

Refuge	Impoundments (acres)	Wetlands (acres)			Riverine (acres)	Lake (acres)	NWI Total (acres)	Water Management Structure(s)
		Seasonal	Temporary	Semi-permanent				
Rabb Lake	0.00	5.53	0.00	2.52	3.47	102.13	113.63	None
Rock Lake	0.00	110.14	78.15	109.99	0.00	831.17	1,129.20	Earthen dike, stop log, and sheet pile spillway
Rose Lake	0.00	28.45	6.74	38.19	0.00	0.00	73.36	2 earthen dikes and 1 rubble spillway
School Section Lake	0.00	0.00	0.31	0.00	0.00	312.56	312.56	Earthen dike and spillway
Sheyenne Lake	564.35	5.06	1.51	0.00	0.00	564.90	570.00	Earthen dam and concrete spillway
Sibley Lake	0.00	0.36	6.68	88.41	0.00	464.96	557.19	None
Silver Lake	0.00	38.96	61.54	86.20	65.19	429.07	624.26	None
Snyder Lake	0.00	22.18	24.40	27.55	0.00	243.82	317.95	Sheet pile spillway, earthen dike, stop log
Springwater	2.83	15.25	0.00	9.59	14.21	0.00	39.05	Earthen dike
Stoney Slough	0.00	57.79	36.40	0.00	0.00	58.01	152.19	3 water control structures
Sunburst Lake	55.78	3.62	8.40	16.57	3.35	49.51	81.35	Earthen dike, metal spillway
Tomahawk	63.12	0.57	3.96	14.03	0.00	65.94	84.49	Earthen dike and spillway
Willow Lake	0.00	81.67	9.47	70.09	0.65	1,164.78	1,326.65	Stop log structure
Wintering River	0.00	9.20	0.09	67.31	0.00	0.00	76.57	4 earthen dikes and sheetpile spillway
Wood Lake	35.52	4.00	6.26	7.12	0.00	40.41	57.78	Masonry water control structure, earthen dike
Total Acres	3,819.57	782.32	481.82	1,169.25	175.57	12,867.08	15,425.06	

WCS = water control structure
Source: Service 2004

Table 11. Water rights filed with the state of North Dakota

Refuge	Water Storage (acre-feet)	Surface Area (acres)	Refuge	Water Storage (acre-feet)	Surface Area (acres)
Appert Lake	965	108	Lost Lake	82	61
Ardoch	5,347	1,150	Maple River	230	130
Bone Hill	114	38	Pleasant Lake	1,166	490
Brumba	375	150	Pretty Rock	688	201
Buffalo Lake	3,125	862	Rabb Lake	251	98
Camp Lake	706	216	Rock Lake	2,829	635
Canfield Lake	872	218	Rose Lake	235	88
Cottonwood Lake	750	200	School Section Lake	2,098	905
Dakota Lake	8,200	1,600	Sheyenne Lake	628	178
Half Way Lake	90	90	Sibley Lake	1,900	487
Hiddenwood	240	112	Silver Lake	1,530	855
Hobart Lake	778	278	Snyder Lake	564	188
Hutchinson Lake	90	90	Springwater	64	16
Johnson Lake	2,590	740	Stoney Slough	1,685	455
Lake George	102	156	Sunburst Lake	66	88
Lake Otis	0	0	Tomahawk	306	63
Lake Patricia	906	278	Willow Lake	7,200	1,200
Lambs Lake	269	111	Wintering River	108	86
Little Goose	138	44	Wood Lake	100	46
Lords Lake	5,252	778	**Total Acres**	**46,391**	**12,256**

Source: Service 2005.

4.3 Cultural Resources

This CCP is not subject to compliance with section 106 of the National Historic Preservation Act. Limited-interest refuges are the rental/lease of non-federally owned land for habitat purposes. The only exception would be if conditions of the agreement specifically identified the protection of cultural resources, which is not the case for the limited-interest refuges.

However, if future federally funded projects on these limited-interest refuges have the potential to affect historic properties, then 106 compliance is necessary.

4.4 Visitor Services

To provide visitor services on the limited-interest refuges, access must be provided by the landowner. If any public activity is allowed, it must be open to the general public. There may be limitations as to the number of participants and seasons of use, but the general public must be given the opportunity to participate because national wildlife refuges are managed by the federal government.

To date, most of the limited-interest refuges have remained closed to all public use. In particular, they historically have been closed to hunting. There has been little public interest in these refuges. Most of these refuges are now posted, but few have entrance signs identifying them by name as is typical on most other national wildlife refuges.

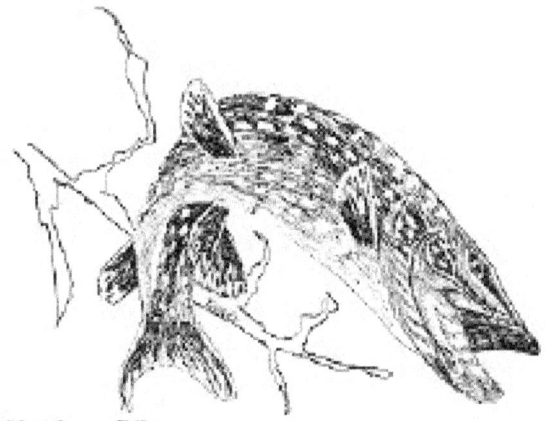

Northern Pike
Tom Kelley/USFWS

During scoping, the state, general public, and some landowners requested opening some refuges to hunting. Increased hunting opportunities and overgrazing by deer and geese, resulting in loss of crops, prompted this request. Trapping has been allowed on a permit-only basis and has become a vital management tool to control unnatural populations of predators that have devastated waterfowl and other grassland nesting birds. Fishing occurs on several refuges and the state has stocked fish in some of the more popular impoundments. Only a few of the refuges have been officially open to public fishing. Numerous requests were made to open these refuges for ice fishing, an extremely popular winter activity in North Dakota.

Other activities such as environmental education and interpretation opportunities, wildlife observation, and photography programs, are nonexistent on the limited-interest refuges. Again, these are private lands so access must be granted by the landowner for an activity to occur. Some landowners expressed interest in establishing environmental education and interpretation programs targeting local schools.

4.5 Socioeconomic Environment

The limited-interest refuges are scattered across a 23-county area with a landbase of 19,970,400 acres. Except for Morton and Grant counties, most counties are located east of the Missouri River. Areas surrounding the limited-interest refuges are typically characterized as rural with an economy and land use based on agriculture. Currently, over 88 percent of the land in these counties is identified as agricultural (table 12).

The state of North Dakota covers 44,156,200 acres. Of this acreage, the Service currently owns 627,116 acres (1.4 percent of the entire state) and has an easement or lease (wetland, grassland, limited-interest) on an additional 1,100,960 acres (3 percent of the entire state). North Dakota ranks 31 in the nation for overall federal land ownership (National Wilderness Institute 1995). Within the 23-county planning area, the Service currently owns 2 percent of the land in national wildlife refuges, WPAs, and National Fish Hatcheries and has various easements on 3.5 percent of lands in this planning area.

Race composition in most of the counties in the Program area is predominantly Caucasian ranging from 50.8 percent (Benson County) to 99.5 percent (Kidder County) (table 13). The next largest group represented is Native American Indian ranging from 0 percent (Emmons) to 48 percent (Benson County). Most of the counties are sparsely populated excluding those with large urban areas such as Grand Forks County and Burleigh County, which encompass the cities of Grand Forks and Bismarck, respectively. Population sizes in 2003 ranged from 2,591 (Kidder County) to 70,987 (Burleigh County). The total population for all counties combined is 296,433, which is 46 percent of North Dakota's 2004 population of 642,200. Population densities range from 1.7/square mile (Grant County) to 42.5/square mile (Burleigh County). Overall, the population of the counties continued to decline between 2000-2003. Population declines ranged from 0.7 percent in Morton County to a decline of 9.9 percent in Sheridan County. Only two counties increased population during this same period: Burleigh County (an increase of 3.3 percent) and Rolette County (an increase of 0.3 percent). The median age varies from 28.9 in Rolette County, to 48.1 in Sheridan County.

The national unemployment rate is 5.0 percent (U.S. Department of Labor 2005). The state of North Dakota's unemployment rate is below the national average at 3.2 percent. The largest employer in the state is the health care and social services (human services) industry employing over 14.1 percent of the state. In 2004, this industry had the largest employment growth in the state (North Dakota Job Service 2004), adding over 1,000 jobs (table 14).

The counties surrounding the limited-interest refuges have an average of 3.1 percent unemployment rate, slightly below the state average. Grant County had the lowest unemployment rate at 1.3 percent, while Rolette County was the highest at 8.2 percent (U.S. Bureau of Census 2000). Human services was the leading industry in 16 of the 23 counties, followed by agriculture (six counties). One county had "entertainment" as the primary industry. The median household income varied between $23,165 in Grant County to $41,309 in Burleigh County (U.S. Bureau of Census 2000).

Table 12 Acres of agricultural and Service-controlled lands by county (% of total land for all listed counties)

County	Land (acres)	Agricultural Lands (acres)	FWS Fee-title (acres)			FmHA Lands (acres)	Wetland Easements (acres)	Grassland Easements (acres)	Limited-interest Refuges in County	Limited-interest Refuge (acres)
			NWR	WPA	NFH					
Barnes	954,880	886,976	246	7,017	110	0	17,312	0	Hobart Lake, Stoney Slough, and Tomahawk	3,151
Benson	883,840	732,870	1,674	7,216	0	1,708	35,195	2,982	Pleasant Lake, Silver Lake (also Rolette), and Wood Lake	4,238
Bottineau	1,068,160	948,475	21,563	2,880	0	471	29,183	0	Lords Lake (also Rolette Co)	1,462
Burleigh	1,045,120	865,524	11,901	11,256	0	2,187	26,063	12,844	Canfield Lake	310
Dickey	723,840	699,450	0	10,042	0	2,584	36,817	9,383	Dakota Lake and Maple River	3,512
Eddy	403,200	348,786	0	4,687	0	417	11,811	0	Johnson Lake	2,008
Emmons	966,400	888,075	0	3,615	0	909	11,492	0	Springwater, Sunburst Lake, and Appert Lake	1,876
Grand Forks	920,320	755,592	680	6,395	0	0	989	0	Little Goose	288
Grant	1,061,760	1,055,729	0	5,383	0	0	5,521	10,331	Pretty Rock	800
Griggs	453,130	279,022	0	3,258	0	101	16,677	0	Sibley Lake	1,077
Kidder	964,640	794,465	6,609	7,404	0	1,222	68,965	9,887	Hutchinson Lake and Lake George	3,569
Lamoure	734,090	676,966	0	5,435	0	955	13,121	0	Bone Hill	640
McHenry	1,199,360	1,125,831	37,122	5,882	0	2,213	29,131	15,272	Cottonwood Lake and Wintering River	1,253

Table 12 Acres of agricultural and Service-controlled lands by county (% of total land for all listed counties)

County	Land (acres)	Agricultural Lands (acres)	FWS Fee-title (acres)			FmHA Lands (acres)	Wetland Easements (acres)	Grassland Easements (acres)	Limited-interest Refuges in County	Limited-interest Refuge (acres)
			NWR	WPA	NFH					
McLean	1,350,400	1,094,748	17,504	12,343	186	73	22,290	7,945	Camp Lake, Hiddenwood, Lake Otis, and Lost Lake	2,438
Morton	1,282,640	1,276,289	0	0	0	375	0	0	Lake Patricia	800
Nelson	628,480	531,591	32	3,541	0	439	37,881	0	Lambs Lake, Johnson Lake, and Rose Lake	2,043
Pierce	661,520	530,628	24	12,750	0	3,906	36,246	1,469	Buffalo Lake	1,540
Ramsey	768,400	636,100	7,710	9,477	0	386	28,730	0	Silver Lake (also Benson Co)	313
Rolette	577,280	507,658	1	5,890	0	361	20,149	0	Ratib Lake, Schol Section Lake, Lords Lake, and Willow Lake	8,616
Sheridan	622,030	468,745	29,737	22,748	0	736	31,427	11,046	Sheyenne Lake	797
Stutsman	1,421,440	1,215,190	17,690	28,277	0	1,259	41,927	11,834	Half Way	160
Towner	656,000	548,774	802	7,241	0	865	24,218	998	Brumba, Rock Lake, and Snyder Lake	9,034
Walsh	820,480	759,381	906	1,736	0	929	8,758	0	Ardoch	2,339
Totals	19,997,440	17,547,848	153,508	184,065	996	20,881	599,158	93,241	99 limited-interest refuges	47,304
Average %		88%	2%			0.1%	2.7%	0.5%		0.2%

Farmers Home Administration Lands.

NWR=national wildlife refuge; WPA=waterfowl production area; NFH=national fish hatchery

Source: US Fish Service FWS.

Table 13. Demographics of the 23 counties within the planning area

County	Population (2003)	Persons per Square Mile	Population Change (2000–2003)	Median Age	Races (% of population)			
					Caucasian	Black	American Indian	Asian
Barnes	11,068	7.9	-5.9%	40.6	97.9	0.5	0.8	0.2
Benson	6,873	5.0	-1.2%	31.4	50.8	0.1	48.0	0
Bottineau	6,808	4.3	-4.6%	43.4	97.2	0.2	1.5	0.2
Burleigh	70,997	42.5	+3.3%	35.6	95.0	0.3	3.3	0.4
Dickey	5,354	5.1	-4.6%	40.7	97.8	0.1	0.3	0.5
Eddy	2,627	4.4	-5.8%	43.8	96.4	0.1	2.4	0.1
Emmons	4,067	2.9	-7.5%	44.5	99.1	0	0.1	0.2
Grand Forks	64,929	46.0	-2.1%	29.2	93.0	1.4	2.3	1.0
Grant	2,689	1.7	-6.2%	46.5	96.9	0	1.7	0.4
Griggs	2,599	3.9	-6.4%	45.8	99.3	0	0.2	0.1
Kidder	2,591	2.0	-6.4%	44.5	99.5	0.2	0.1	0.1
Lamoure	4,509	4.1	-4.0%	43.3	99.2	0	0.2	0.1
McHenry	5,739	3.2	-4.4%	43.0	98.7	0.1	0.4	0
McLean	9,011	4.4	-4.0%	44.1	92.5	0	5.9	0.1
Morton	25,191	18.1	-0.7%	37.4	95.8	0.2	2.4	0.3
Nelson	3,464	3.8	-7.0%	47.2	98.6	0.1	0.3	0.3
Pierce	4,325	4.6	-4.2%	42.9	98.5	0.1	0.7	0.2
Ramsey	11,746	10.2	-3.7%	39.5	92.3	0.2	5.4	0.3
Rolette	13,760	15.2	+0.4%	28.9	25.1	0.1	73.0	0.1
Sheridan	1,572	1.8	-9.9%	48.1	99.2	0.1	0.4	0
Stutsman	21,388	9.9	-8.0%	39.6	97.5	0.3	0.9	0.4
Towner	2,712	2.8	-7.3%	44.0	97.3	0.1	2.1	0.1
Walsh	11,891	9.7	-5.4%	40.9	94.9	0.3	1.0	0.2

Source: U.S. Bureau of Census 2003

Table 14. Employment data for counties in the Program area

County	Primary Industry	% Employment	Secondary Industry	% Employment	% Unemployment (2000)	Median Household Income ($/year)
Barnes	Human Services	27.4	Retail	11.9	2.9	31,166
Benson	Human Services	23.4	Agriculture	15.8	7.4	26,688
Bottineau	Human Services	23.8	Agriculture	16.1	2.7	29,853
Burleigh	Human Services	23.2	Retail	13.0	2.5	41,300
Dickey	Human Services	24.5	Agriculture	17.3	2.5	29,231
Eddy	Human Services	27.4	Agriculture	19.6	2.7	28,642
Emmons	Agriculture	28.0	Human Services	19.8	1.9	26,119
Grand Forks	Human Services	29.8	Retail	13.6	2.9	35,785
Grant	Agriculture	33.5	Human Services	20.1	1.3	29,165
Griggs	Human Services	20.4	Agriculture	16.0	1.9	29,572
Kidder	Agriculture	30.1	Human Services	21.7	2.7	25,399
Lamoure	Agriculture	23.3	Human Services	17.4	1.6	29,707
McHenry	Agriculture	20.5	Human Services	18.9	2.9	27,274
McLean	Human Services	21.5	Agriculture	16.7	3.2	32,387
Morton	Human Services	23.0	Retail	12.1	2.6	37,028
Nelson	Human Services	27.7	Agriculture	16.3	1.8	28,892
Pierce	Human Services	25.1	Agriculture	16.5	2.4	26,524
Ramsey	Human Services	25.9	Retail	15.9	4.5	35,600
Rolette	Human Services	34.7	Entertainment	9.8	8.2	26,232
Sheridan	Agriculture	35.0	Human Services	16.0	3.9	24,450
Stutsman	Human Services	26.8	Manufacturing	11.4	2.2	33,848
Towner	Entertainment	22.1	Agriculture	20.7	1.4	32,740
Walsh	Human Services	27.1	Agriculture	16.1	4.0	33,845

Source: U.S. Bureau of Census 2002

Chapter 5. Environmental Consequences

5.1 Effects Common to all Alternatives

The following considerations apply to all future actions, regardless of the specific goals, objectives, and strategies that would be used to achieve the vision for the Program.

Landowner Rights

Landowners would always have the right to determine their level of participation, if any, in the activities and projects proposed outside the intent of the current flowage and/or refuge limited-interest refuge agreement (see section 2.3 for discussion).

Landowners would be provided information on available compensated programs for further protecting wildlife habitat, but no response would be required unless the landowner is willing to participate. For a discussion on fee-title actions, see the following information on the Service's land acquisition policy.

The Service would ensure that any activities associated with the Program would not adversely impact adjacent landowners including activities that would detract from the value of their property. Any landowners adjacent to lands owned or managed by the Service would retain all the rights, privileges, and responsibilities of private land ownership.

Service Land Acquisition Policy

The Service acquires lands and interests in lands consistent with legislation or other congressional guidelines and executive orders, for the conservation of fish and wildlife and to provide wildlife-dependent public use for education and recreational purposes. The Service policy is to acquire land only when other protective means, such as zoning and regulation, are not appropriate, available, or effective. When the Service acquires land, it acquires fee title (all property rights) only if lesser property interests (such as conservation easements, leases, or cooperative agreements) are not suitable to achieve resource objectives.

It is Service policy to acquire the minimum interest necessary to reach Program goals and objectives. Any Service acquisition of lands, regardless of the type (easement or fee-title purchase) would be from willing sellers only. Written offers to willing sellers would be based on a professional appraisal of the property using recent sales of comparable properties in the area. Landowners would in no way be coerced into selling their land or any interest in their land. The Service recognizes that every landowner within or adjacent to an existing or proposed national wildlife refuge has the right:

- to retain all privileges and responsibilities of private ownership;
- to sell their land to anyone of their choice;
- not to sell their land;
- to receive a fair market value for any property sought for purchase by the U.S. Fish and Wildlife Service;
- to control access to their land;
- to be heard and to provide input on management plans for neighboring refuge lands;
- to be informed on a regular basis about refuge management activities.

The Refuge Revenue Sharing Act of June 15, 1935, as amended, provides for annual payments to counties or the lowest unit of government that collects and distributes taxes based on acreage and value of national wildlife refuge lands located with the county. The monies for these payments come from two sources: (1) net receipts from the sale of products from national wildlife refuge appropriations; and (2) annual congressional appropriations, as authorized by the 1978 amendment, which were intended to make up the difference between the net receipts from the Refuge Revenue Sharing Fund and the total amount due to local units of government.

Maintenance of Roads and Existing Rights-of-Way

State, county, and townships would retain maintenance obligations for roads and associated rights-of-way under their jurisdiction within refuge boundaries. Existing rights-of-way and terms of other easements would continue to be honored. New rights-of-way and easements would be considered in relation to the existing refuge and/or flowage limited-interest refuge agreements, System regulations, landowner compliance, and likely impacts to wildlife resources.

Environmental Justice

Environmental justice refers to the principle that all citizens and communities are entitled to:

- equal protection from environmental occupational health or safety hazards;
- equal access to natural resources and;
- equal participation in the environmental and natural resource policy formulation process.

On February 11, 1994, President Clinton issued Executive Order (EO) 12898: "Federal Actions to Address Environmental Justice in Minority Populations and low Income Populations." The purpose of this Order was to focus attention of federal agencies on human environmental health and to address inequities that may occur in the distribution of costs/benefits, land use patterns, hazardous material transport or facility siting, allocation and consumption of resources, access to information, planning, and decision making, etc.

The mission of the U.S. Fish and Wildlife Service is working with others to conserve, protect, and enhance fish and wildlife and their habitats for the continuing benefit of the American people. The environmental justice strategy of the Service extends this mission by seeking to ensure that all segments of the human population have equal access to America's fish and wildlife resources, as well as equal access to information that would enable them to participate meaningfully in activities and policy shaping.

Within the spirit and intent of EO 12898, no minority or low income populations would be impacted by any Service action under any alternative.

5.2 Summary of Effects by Alternative

The following section and table 15 provide an analysis of effects resulting from no action (alternative A) and the preferred alternative (alternative B).

Alternative A (No Action)

Existing Program management would be the focus of this alternative. As in the past, there would be no additional staff or funding provided to manage the limited-interest refuges. Any activities conducted on the refuges would continue to be incidental to other funded programs, or funding would be acquired through partnerships with conservation organizations. Hunting on the entire limited-interest refuge and any activities that occur on the water would be controlled by the Service.

There would be continual loss of upland habitats due to development. In particular, native prairie would be permanently lost as land uses change and areas become developed.

Those refuges which contain any high hazard dams would be repaired or replaced to ensure public safety. However, most other water management structures would continue to deteriorate due to lack of available funding. There would be a continued loss of wetland management of impoundments, reducing the production of desirable wetland habitats needed for international migratory bird use. Natural wetlands would remain unprotected, potentially reducing the availability of nutritional food sources and habitats needed for nesting and migratory birds and other wetland-dependent wildlife.

Current visitor services programs such as permit-only trapping, limited hunting and fishing, would continue if they remain compatible and resources are available to manage them. No additional public use activities would be pursued unless the Service was approached by a willing landowner. Additional uses would not be allowed unless it was determined to be compatible with the refuge purposes, and if funding is available to manage the use.

No refuges would be divested, further straining available resources for the Program.

Table 15. Summary of environmental consequences for management alternatives

Issue	Alternative A (Current Management—No Action)	Alternative B (Enhance the North Dakota Limited-interest Program)
Wetland Management	*Biodiversity:* Continued loss of biodiversity due to potential draining or siltation of wetlands.	*Biodiversity:* Work with willing landowners to restore and enhance biodiversity through the protection of over 2,500 acres of natural wetlands.
	Water Level Management: Continued loss of ability to manage impoundments according to modern practices.	*Water Level Management:* Properly manage impoundments for maximum production of waterfowl and other wetland-dependent birds.
	Siltation: No program to actively work with farmers to reduce sedimentation. Wetlands would be lost as silt is deposited by runoff from surrounding agricultural uses.	*Siltation:* Restore upland vegetation and capture and reduce siltation, preserving wetlands.
	Waterfowl: Dominant focus; lack of management and protection of wetlands and nesting habitat. No guarantee of upland cover for nesting and continued loss of wetlands and water level management capabilities due to dilapidating structures; minimal production.	*Waterfowl:* Dominant focus; increase ability to carry out proper water level management, protect natural wetlands, and provide quality nesting cover. Maximize success of nesting waterfowl and brood survival.
Upland Management	*Biodiversity:* No concerted effort to compensate landowners for upland protections. Impact: Continued loss of biodiversity, in particular native prairie, due to upland development and intense farming practices.	*Biodiversity:* Work with willing landowners to negotiate added compensations for restoring and enhancing biodiversity through upland habitat protection.
	Grassland-dependent Species: No habitat protection of upland vegetation. Little to no habitat available for nesting waterfowl or grassland-dependent birds; minimal production and recruitment.	*Grassland-dependent Species:* Restore upland nesting bird habitat. Impact: Nesting success of waterfowl and grassland-dependent birds would increase ensuring greater success and survival.
	Native Prairie: No concerted effort to compensate landowners for native prairie protection. Continued and permanent loss of "true" native prairie habitat.	*Native Prairie:* Give highest priority to native prairie habitat protection through compensated programs. Potential to protect over 14,000 acres of native prairie.

Table 15. Summary of environmental consequences for management alternatives

Issue	Alternative A (Current Management—No Action)	Alternative B (Enhance the North Dakota Limited-interest Program)
Visitor Services	*Access:* Little to no access would be provided on these privately owned refuges. Few visitor services programs would be provided.	*Access:* Negotiations with willing landowners to provide access for expanded public use activities and education of visitors about the Program and the System.
	Hunting: No additional hunting would be permitted due to lack of resources; crop damage issues would not be addressed and this continued refuge status would continue to concentrate harvestable animal populations further damaging crops and costing landowners significant losses each year.	*Hunting:* Determine compatibility and willingness of landowners to provide access for hunting (except ducks and certain geese species). Crop damage issue addressed while providing increased hunting opportunities for the general public.
	Trapping: Trapping would continue on a permit-only basis focusing on predator management for the protection of migratory birds.	*Trapping:* Continuing the predator management program while ensuring trappers focus their future efforts on those refuges with habitat desired by nesting waterfowl and grassland birds will improve nesting success and production. The program will also address wildlife damage to water management structures and desirable habitats. Water level management will be enhanced and desirable habitat, such as riparian areas, will be protected. In addition, the trapping program will be reexamined when the International Association of Fish and Wildlife Agencies makes its recommendations for Best Management Practices. Their research and resulting recommendations will only improve this program.
	Nonconsumptive Uses: No programs would be provided for wildlife viewing and photography, environmental education and interpretation. There would be a continued lack of understanding of the purposes of the Program along with a missed opportunity to further educate the public about the System.	*Nonconsumptive Uses:* Determine compatibility and willingness of landowners to provide access for wildlife viewing and photography, environmental education and interpretation, increasing public use while providing a widespread opportunity to educate the public about the Program and the System.
	Natural Resources: No monitoring of the impacts of public disturbance to wildlife.	*Natural Resources:* Monitor wildlife responses to changes in public uses to determine and modify negative impacts.
	Fishing: Additional fishing opportunities would not be actively pursued for the general public.	
Partnerships	*Landowners:* Little to no contact with limited-interest refuge landowners. The Program will never reach its full potential.	*Landowners:* At a minimum, landowners would be provided annual updates on the Program and any opportunities for them to receive compensation for added protections of upland and wetland habitats. Landowners would become true partners in the Program. This would result in a greater chance of success if these landowners are fully engaged. Habitat would be maintained or restored.

Table 15. Summary of environmental consequences for management alternatives

Issue	Alternative A (Current Management—No Action)	Alternative B (Enhance the North Dakota Limited-interest Program)
	Other Partners: Partnerships would be developed incidental to needs and common interests. Loss of potential funds and services	*Other Partners:* Actively identify and coordinate with potential partners to achieve common goals that enhance and support the Program. Extend existing resources, including funding and knowledge.
Administration	Continued loss of biodiversity and ability to manage impoundments for wildlife.	Ability to partner with willing landowners to address management and maintenance issues and protection of natural resources for migratory birds and other wildlife.
Divestiture	Even though some have no potential to ever support the goals of the System, all refuges would be retained. Program resources would be further strained with little to no gain of wildlife habitat. Integrity of the System would be affected by retaining lands that do no support the goal of the System.	Six refuges would be divested based on loss of habitat and wildlife values due to development or the ability and willingness of the state to continue to manage limited-interest refuge lands as state Wildlife Management Areas. This would support the integrity of the System and ensure the best use of available resources.

Alternative B (Preferred Alternative)

Alternative B would emphasize taking a critical look at the needs and benefits of the limited-interest refuges. Relationships with landowners would be enhanced and programs would be available to willing landowners providing additional compensation and protection for those refuge lands identified as having the most critical habitats.

All refuge water management structures would be evaluated for needed repairs and replacements. Necessary work would be completed by local contractors and supplies would be acquired locally providing economic benefits to the local communities.

Several water management structures need repairs.

Managing stations would plan and initiate water level management programs on these impoundments to ensure maximum production of desirable aquatic plants and invertebrates utilized by nesting and migratory waterbirds, in particular, waterfowl. Maintaining water features on landowners' properties would maintain or increase land value due to the aesthetics and opportunities for wildlife-dependent recreation, such as fishing and birdwatching, a more reliable source of stockwater for livestock.

Landowners would be encouraged to use Best Management Practices (BMPs) for farming operations to reduce siltation and contamination of impoundments and natural wetlands. Managing stations would ensure landowners are provided the necessary BMP information provided by the U.S. Department of Agriculture.

Refuge staff would partner with willing landowners and the NDGF to evaluate many of the refuges for opportunities for public use. Affected landowners would need to provide access to the general public and the Service would monitor impacts to wildlife and landowners. Increased hunting, fishing, and other recreational opportunities would provide an economic benefit to the surrounding areas. Four seasonal law enforcement officers would be recruited for managing and monitoring these new public uses, while ensuring visitor and landowner safety.

Six refuges would be divested ensuring the existing and added program resources are utilized on those refuges with potential to become national wildlife refuges in more than name only. Refuges with extensive loss of biodiversity that no longer meet their purpose or the goals of National Wildlife Refuge System and those that are currently owned and/or managed by the state (easements revoked), would be divested. No wildlife habitat would be lost on those areas that would be managed by the NDGF. Recreational opportunities would continue or expand providing quality of life and economic benefits to the local communities. Some refuges would be divested giving all rights back to the landowners or a landowner designated managing interest excluding the water rights, which would be relinquished to the State. The Service would ensure that any water management structures meet federal and state safety standards prior to divestiture and transfer.

Chapter 6. Management Direction

Note: Comprehensive conservation plans provide long-term guidance for management decisions and set forth goals, objectives, and strategies needed to accomplish refuge purposes and identify the U.S. Fish and Wildlife Service's best estimate of future needs. These plans detail program planning levels that are sometimes substantially above current budget allocations, and, as such, are primarily for Service strategic planning and program prioritization purposes. The plans do not constitute a commitment for staffing increases, operational and maintenance increases, or funding for future land acquisition.

6.1 Introduction

During the next 15 years, the objectives and strategies presented below will guide the management of these refuges and future allocations. The Service will implement this CCP with assistance from willing landowners, existing and new partner agencies and organizations, and the public. No action taken in this plan will have any negative impacts on endangered species (see "Appendix F, Section 7 Biological Evaluation").

Although a number of needs were identified during the planning process, there are no assurances that any projects would be fully or even partially funded. However, within every planning effort, there are opportunities to examine current allocations of funding and resources and determine the best available uses based on a more comprehensive planning evaluation of critical needs.

6.2 Refuge Divestiture Proposals

To date, over 98 percent of limited-interest refuge lands remain in private ownership. Within the approved acquisition boundary, 99 percent of the acres remain in private ownership. For all practical purposes, after 70 years, the Service is still at a starting point for attempting to give some assurance that these lands can retain the qualities desirable in a national wildlife refuge. To that end, the Service first examined each refuge to determine if it should be retained in the National Wildlife Refuge System.

A Regional Team of managers, planners, and regional directorate convened to develop a Region 6 model for determining, as part of the CCP process, whether a refuge should be retained in the System (see "Appendix G, Divestiture Model"). Factors were considered in evaluating each refuge for retention, such as (1) ability to meet the goals of the System, (2) ability to meet the refuge purpose(s), (3) existing biodiversity including native habitat, (4) associated conservation lands, and (5) current state and other federal management of these areas. The limited-interest refuges planning team utilized this model in their decision making. The entire team reviewed land status maps and listened to a presentation by each managing station describing the negative impacts and potential of each refuge. Land status maps displayed associated wetlands and other habitats as well as other Service and state interests adjacent to or surrounding each refuge. These included Service wetland or grassland easements, WPAs, NDGF Wildlife Management Areas, and other NWRs.

Since the 1950s, when dozens of limited-interest refuges were divested, no attempt has been made to evaluate each refuge comprehensively to determine its capability to meet the goals of the System. In addition to refuges lacking biodiversity due to negative impacts, the Service also examined refuges currently owned or managed by the state or another federal agency. Because there will be no opportunity for the Service to acquire any additional interests in these lands, there is no logical reason for the Service to continue to retain any interest, particularly on state-owned lands currently being managed for wildlife. Additionally, the limited-interest refuges cannot be equated to a similar fee-title refuge where the Service has full management control.

In the past 70 years, the Service has acquired additional rights, primarily through acquisition, on only 1 percent of the approved acquisition boundaries. In addition, dozens of other limited-interest refuges have been divested since this Program was established. Most recently in 1999, Lake Elsie National Wildlife Refuge was divested due to habitat losses and issues similar to the following divestiture proposals.

Six refuges are being proposed for consideration for divestiture:

- Bone Hill NWR
- Camp Lake NWR
- Cottonwood Lake NWR
- Lake Patricia NWR
- School Section Lake NWR
- Sheyenne Lake NWR

During scoping, the Service received numerous requests from landowners to divest several of the limited-interest refuges. Each refuge was considered during discussions on divestiture. For example, the Service received requests to divest both Bone Hill and Sheyenne Lake NWRs, which are now on the divestiture list.

Several meetings were held with the landowners of Camp Lake NWR in the past to discuss divestiture and there is support.

Lake Patricia is primarily owned and managed by the state and has long supported divestiture.

Sheyenne Lake NWR is owned by the BOR and managed by the state under a 1980s agreement. The Service is present in name only and there will be no loss of habitat for wildlife from what occurs there today. BOR and the state support divestiture of Sheyenne Lake.

Cottonwood Lake received one comment against divestiture during scoping, but divestiture has been supported by the majority of the landowners in the past. The state also is interested in managing this popular fishery.

No comments were received for School Section Lake during scoping. However, the state owns the upland areas surrounding the lake and supports divestiture and acquiring management.

Each of these refuges were established either by executive order or other legislation. No approval from the Migratory Bird Conservation Commission was requested at the time these refuges were established. Although the specific details for divesting each of these refuges will be addressed when the CCP is implemented, the Service plans to provide the Migratory Bird Conservation Commission the proposals for divestiture and ask for its concurrence. The final approval for divestiture will require an act of Congress.

The following proposals provide a brief history and justification for considering each of the six refuges for divestiture.

Bone Hill NWR

Proposal and Justification

Three perpetual refuge and flowage easement agreements were signed by private landowners in LaMoure County in 1935. On May 10, 1939, an executive order was signed by President Roosevelt establishing these lands and waters as Bone Hill National Wildlife Refuge (figure 18). An approved acquisition boundary was designated within and around these limited-interest refuge lands totaling 640 acres to serve as a "refuge and breeding grounds for migratory birds." Because the Service never acquired any of these lands fee title, the purpose of this limited-interest refuge land is contained in the easement agreements including (a) water conservation, (b) drought relief, (c) a wildlife demonstration unit, and (d) a closed refuge and reservation for migratory birds and other wildlife.

The land use and activities surrounding the constructed and natural wetlands on the Bone Hill NWR make management of these wetlands for the benefit of migratory birds impractical. Most of the refuge habitat has been converted for tillage agriculture. Some of the refuge, including the area around the main, constructed impoundment, is currently being used as a feedlot to raise domestic elk. As a result, the remnant areas of grass or native vegetation are severely overgrazed.

In addition, there is a farm house and associated outbuildings on the refuge along with a fertilizer plant. For this refuge to fulfill its intended purposes according to the executive order, the elk farm and the fertilizer plant would have to be removed and the grass areas restored, which is unrealistic to expect.

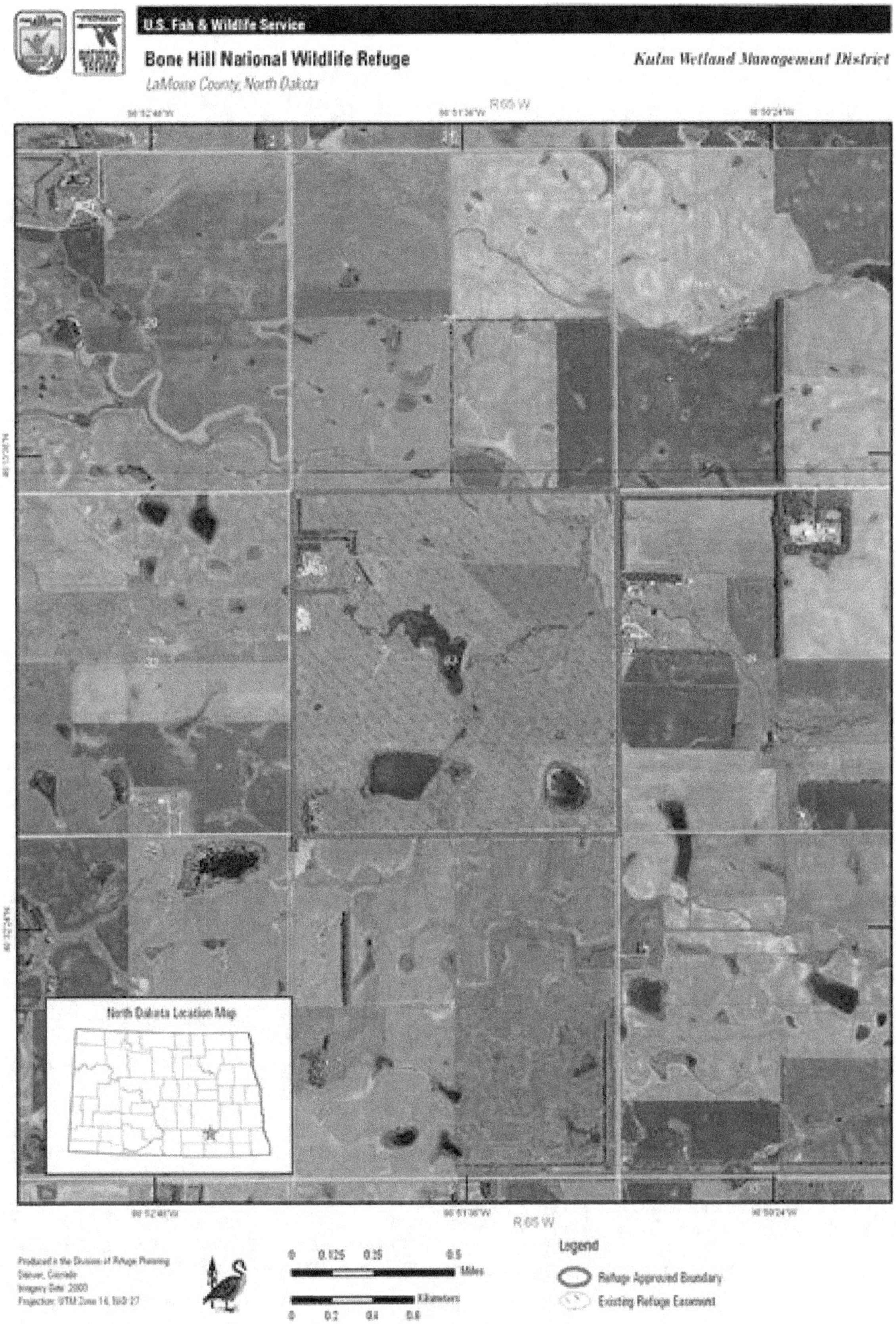

U.S. Fish & Wildlife Service

Bone Hill National Wildlife Refuge

Kulm Wetland Management District

LaMoure County, North Dakota

North Dakota Location Map

Produced in the Division of Refuge Planning
Denver, Colorado
Imagery Date: 2000
Projection: UTM Zone 14, NAD 27

0   0.125   0.25   0.5
                          Miles

0   0.2   0.4   0.6
                          Kilometers

Legend

⬭ Refuge Approved Boundary

⬭ Existing Refuge Easement

Figure 18. Bone Hill NWR

Additionally, the Service has no authority to restore these uplands under the current agreements.

Recommendation: Divest this limited-interest refuge, revoke all the refuge and flowage easement agreements, and voluntary relinquish the water rights to the State. Negotiate with the state to manage the water resource.

Camp Lake NWR

Proposal and Justification

In 1935 and 1936, seven perpetual and one revocable refuge and flowage easement agreements were signed by the state and private landowners in McLean County. On May 10, 1939, an executive order was signed by President Roosevelt establishing these lands and waters as Camp Lake National Wildlife Refuge (figure 19). An approved acquisition boundary was designated within and around these limited-interest refuge lands totaling 1,212 acres to serve as a "refuge and breeding grounds for migratory birds." Because the Service never acquired any of these lands fee title, the purpose of this limited-interest refuge land is contained in the refuge and flowage easement agreements including (a) water conservation, (b) drought relief, (c) a wildlife demonstration unit, and (d) a closed refuge and reservation for migratory birds and other wildlife.

In 1974 the limited-interest refuge for refuge rights contained in Section 36 of T150N and R80W and owned by the North Dakota State Land Commissioner, acting on behalf of the Board of University and School Lands, was revoked on the non-meandered acreage. This revocation reduced the limited-interest refuge acreage to approximately 585 acres.

The current approximate boundary of the refuge consists of the E½SE¼ of Section 25, T150N and R80W, the waters of Camp and Strawberry lakes in Section 36, the SE¼ of Section 35, T150N and R80W, and the E½ of Section 2, T149N and R80W.

Camp and Strawberry lakes are controlled in elevation by a dam and water control structure located at the south end of Strawberry Lake. Currently, the uplands within the refuge boundary in Section 25 and the SE¼ of Section 2

Boat docks and 149 cabins surround the lake on Camp Lake NWR.

are utilized for agriculture. The uplands in the NE¼ of Section 2 and in Section 35 are dominated by cabins and recreational features.

The lands and waters in and around Camp Lake NWR have always been a popular recreational area, even prior to establishment of the national wildlife refuge. Recreational development on Strawberry Lake increased in the 1950s. Today development consists of over 149 cabins, a beach, resort, docks, boat ramp, a road system, and a recreational services district. The human impact of the cabins, boats, sewage, swimming, personal water craft, and recreational use on the refuge has greatly reduced or eliminated the ability of this area to meet its purpose and any goals of the System. In addition, with the revocation of the state's limited-interest refuge, the Service no longer has any means to regulate human disturbance immediately adjacent to and around the entire periphery of the lakes in Section 36.

The purpose for which this refuge was established was based on attributes it possessed and exhibited at the time of establishment. Those attributes were relative and conditionally linked to the original contiguous size and shape characteristics. The government's interest in this refuge no longer retains those size and shape characteristics. Most importantly, the development of dozens of lakeside cabins and the supporting recreational facilities have rendered this refuge incapable of ever meeting the purpose for which it was originally established.

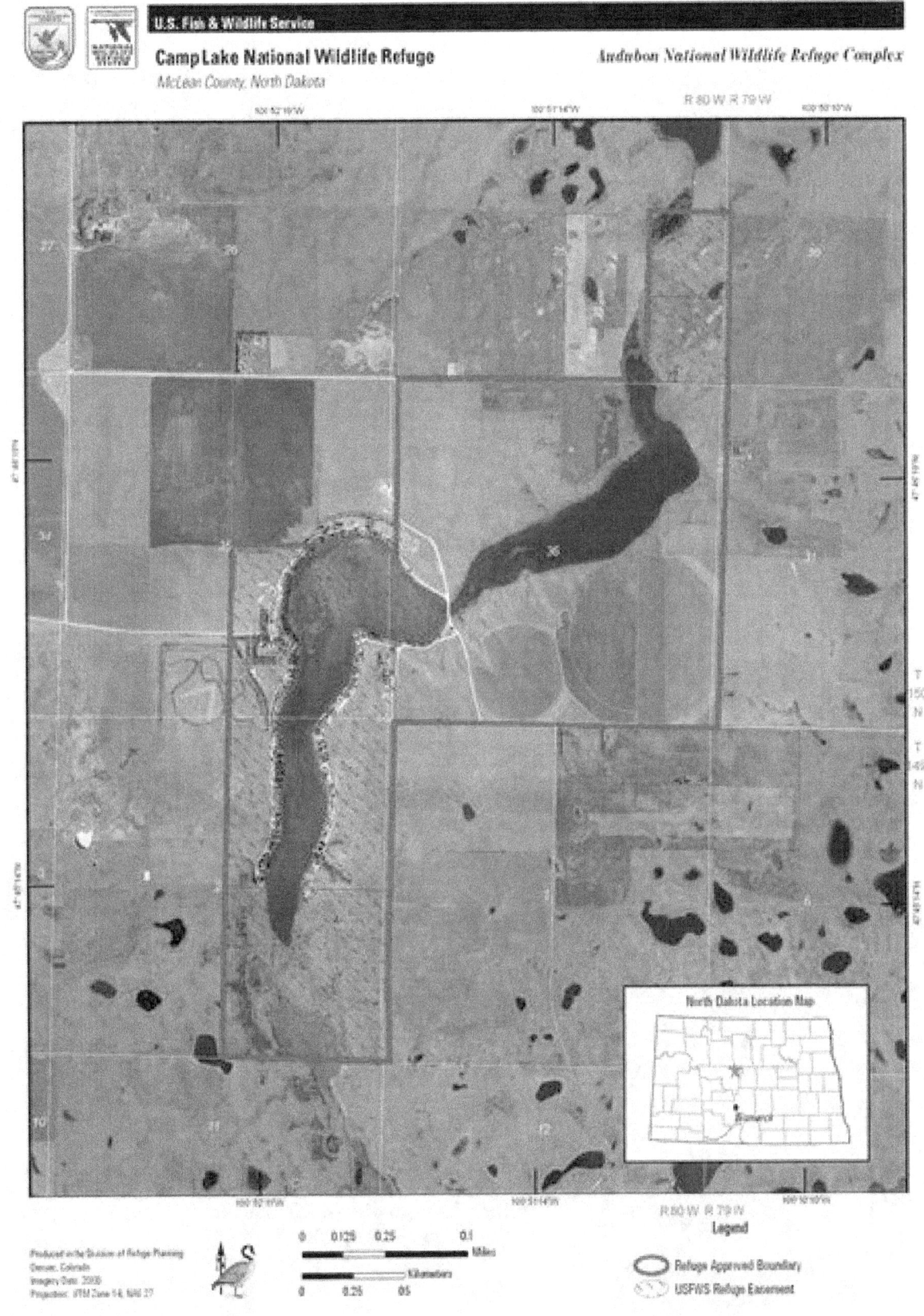

Figure 19. Camp Lake NWR

Recommendation: Divest the limited-interest refuge, revoke the refuge and flowage easements, and voluntarily relinquish the water rights. Transfer management of the dam to the McLean County Water Resource District or the Strawberry Lake Recreation District.

Cottonwood Lake NWR

Proposal and Justification

Seven perpetual refuge and flowage easement agreements were signed in McHenry County by private landowners between 1936 and 1987. On June 12, 1939, an executive order was signed by President Roosevelt establishing these lands and waters as Cottonwood Lake National Wildlife Refuge (figure 20). An approved acquisition boundary was designated within and around these limited-interest refuge lands totaling 1,013 acres to serve as a "refuge and breeding grounds for migratory birds." Because the Service never acquired any of these lands fee title, the purpose of this limited-interest refuge land is contained in the refuge and flowage easement agreements including (a) water conservation, (b) drought relief, (c) a wildlife demonstration unit, and (d) a closed refuge and reservation for migratory birds and other wildlife.

Cottonwood Lake is the principle water area on the refuge encompassing about 260 acres. It receives water from runoff to the west and a diversion ditch from the east. The boundary consists of over 500 acres of uplands in Section 28 and parts of Section 21 and Section 33. Most

of the Cottonwood Lake boundary is the high watermark on nearly two-thirds of the basin.

The uplands are in poor condition for waterfowl and other migratory birds. Nearly all uplands have been cultivated at some time and all have planted tree lines and shelterbelts, as well as trees that escaped cultivation, dotting the landscape. Three roads either bisect the refuge or transverse its boundary. There are two large farmsteads within the boundary, two permanent homes, and a seasonal mobile home.

The water control structure and spillway are in disrepair and do not function as originally planned. The diversion ditch to the east is filled with sediment, has become overgrown with brush and trees, and only functions under flood conditions. Local residents poured concrete into the water control structure and raised the lake level by 1 foot. The spillway in most years is nonfunctional and has blown out several times in the past.

The NDGF completed repairs on the structure to maintain the fishery. It also constructed a boat ramp on the west shoreline on other private land and encouraged fishing. This is the main fishing area for the rural residents of the Butte area. Historically, the residents have worked to keep the lake deep so as to maintain the fishery. The state periodically stocks the lake with game fish.

Some local anglers want the lake maintained for recreation. Attempts to plug the water control structure and spillway have occurred several times over the years. There also have been attempts to divert more water to the lake when possible. Any attempt to manage the lake for migratory bird use was abandoned in the 1960s due to local resident hostilities.

By keeping the lake deep, the habitat value for waterfowl has diminished. Little if any submerged vegetation has been noted over the years and little emergent vegetation has established itself along the shore. Previous managers have noted the area gets little use by waterfowl or other water birds except for small groups of birds during migration. Most times nesting birds are disturbed by the numerous boats using the area.

Cottonwood Lake NWR

Laura King/USFWS

Figure 20. Cottonwood Lake NWR

Wildlife use has been severely compromised leaving limited remaining biological values combined with long-standing law enforcement issues, which will undoubtedly increase as future developments (uses the Service does not regulate) continue.

Recommendation: Divest the limited-interest refuge and revoke the refuge and flowage easement agreements. Voluntarily relinquish the water right to the State, which should be allowed to continue to operate the area as a recreational fishery. Negotiations should be initiated with the state to determine if a trade for management responsibilities for Cottonwood Lake NWR could be exchanged for management rights on another limited-interest refuge with greater wildlife values. The Service should concentrate its efforts on other neighboring Service interests with greater potential, including the Cottonwood WPA and the Wintering River NWR (another limited-interest refuge).

Lake Patricia NWR

Proposal and Justification

Five refuge and flowage easement agreements were signed by private landowners and the state in Morton County between 1936 and 1938. Two of these agreements with the state, totaling 800 acres, are revocable; the remaining four agreements are perpetual. On June 12, 1939, an executive order was signed by President Roosevelt establishing these lands as Lake Patricia National Wildlife Refuge (figure 21). An approved acquisition boundary was designated within and around these limited-interest refuge lands totaling 1,434 acres to serve as a "...refuge and breeding grounds for migratory birds." Because the Service never acquired any of these lands fee title, the purpose of this limited-interest refuge land is contained in the refuge easement agreements including (a) water conservation, (b) drought relief, (c) a wildlife demonstration unit, and (d) a closed refuge and reservation for migratory birds and other wildlife.

In 1949, the state of North Dakota revoked one limited-interest refuge agreement for 640 acres. These lands and waters are located in the center of the refuge in Section 36. The state has an additional 160 acre area in Section 26, where the easement has yet to be revoked.

The major feature of this refuge as established was Lake Patricia. The majority of this lake is located in Section 36 and is no longer protected by a limited-interest refuge agreement. The revoked lands surrounding Lake Patricia in Section 36, are managed as wildlife habitat by the NDGF. The remaining uplands still covered by a limited-interest agreement, are used for agricultural purposes and are of marginal wildlife value.

In 1955, the U.S. Fish and Wildlife Service entered into a management agreement with NDGF to manage the entire refuge. The long-range plan was for the state to work with the landowners within the refuge to acquire state agreements similar to the federal refuge and flowage easement agreements. This was necessary as the federal agreements could not be transferred to the state. The state has been unable to obtain these agreements; therefore, they requested the federal agreements remain in effect. Nevertheless, the state has continued to manage most of the refuge as a Wildlife Management Area.

The purpose for which this refuge was originally established was based on attributes it possessed and exhibited at the time of establishment. Those attributes were relative and conditionally linked to the original size and features. This refuge no longer retains those characteristics. The majority of refuge and migratory bird breeding use exists or is associated with the part of Lake Patricia where the limited-interest refuge agreement was revoked. It would be more appropriate for the state, which owns and currently manages most of the lands within the refuge boundary, to take jurisdiction over the area.

Recommendation: Divest the limited-interest refuge, revoke the refuge and flowage easement agreements, and voluntarily relinquish the water rights and transfer management of the structure to the State. Allow the State to continue to operate the area as a Wildlife Management Area. Negotiations with the State will include determining if these management responsibilities could be exchanged for management rights on another limited-interest refuge with greater wildlife values.

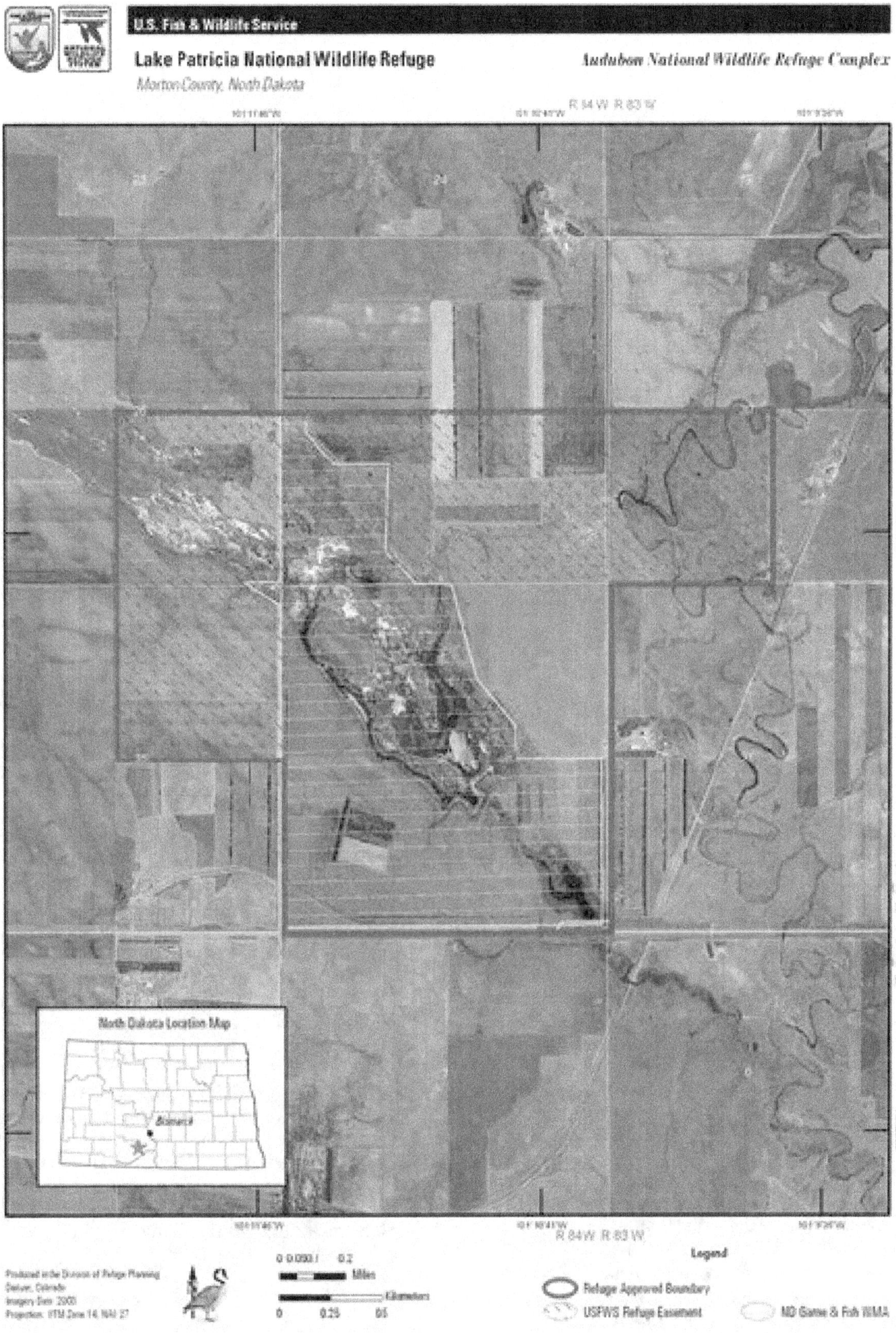

U.S. Fish & Wildlife Service

Lake Patricia National Wildlife Refuge
Morton County, North Dakota

Audubon National Wildlife Refuge Complex

Produced in the Division of Refuge Planning
Denver, Colorado
Imagery Date: 2003
Projection: UTM Zone 14, NAD 27

Legend

◯ Refuge Approved Boundary

USFWS Refuge Easement

◯ ND Game & Fish WMA

Figure 21. Lake Patricia NWR

School Section Lake NWR

Proposal and Justification

One revocable and two perpetual refuge and/or flowage easement agreements were signed between 1935 and 1937 in Rolette County by private landowners and the state. On December 21, 1948, these lands and waters became School Section Lake National Wildlife Refuge (figure 22) under the authority of the Act of August 14, 1946, a precursor the Fish and Wildlife Coordination Act. An approved acquisition boundary was designated within and around these limited-interest refuge lands totaling 680 acres. Because the Service never acquired any of these lands fee title, the purpose of this limited-interest refuge is contained in the refuge and/or flowage easement agreements including (a) water conservation, (b) drought relief, (c) a wildlife demonstration unit, and (d) a closed refuge and reservation for migratory birds and other wildlife.

In 1996, the revocable refuge and flowage easement signed by the state was cancelled by them. The agreement covered the land described as T163N, R72W, Section 16, frac. ALL (also described as Gov. Lots 1 thru 9, S½SE¼). This area (tract 2a) was about 383 acres of upland surrounding the 261-acre lake in Section 16. The only remaining upland within the existing limited-interest refuge boundary is in another agreement described as T163N, R72W, Section 9, Lot 4 comprised of 37 acres. The original refuge consisting of 680 acres has been reduced to 297 acres. Of the remaining refuge, 88 percent is composed of the 261-acre lake. The government no longer has jurisdiction to prevent human disturbance immediately adjacent to and around the entire periphery of the lake.

Within Section 16, the legal boundary of the lake is the now the legal boundary of the remaining limited-interest refuge. To enforce provisions of the limited-interest refuge, the legal boundary must be adequately signed. For the legal boundary to be signed, it must be identifiable on the landscape. The water levels in the lake fluctuate seasonally and from year to year. Thus, this legal boundary is not evident on the landscape. For this reason, management personnel responsible for enforcement of the limited-interest refuge provisions have been reluctant to place signs that would identify the modified boundary. In addition, a lake does not make a refuge. The diversity of habitats, found both on the lake and in the surrounding uplands are necessary for adequate protection, diversity, enhancement, and management of a balance of habitats necessary for healthy wildlife populations, in particular federal trust species such as nesting waterfowl and grassland birds.

The purpose for which this refuge was originally established was based on attributes it possessed and exhibited at the time of establishment. Those attributes were relative and conditionally linked to the original size and features. This refuge no longer retains those characteristics. Thus, in its downsized state, it no longer meets the purpose for which it was originally established.

Recommendation: Divest the limited-interest refuge and revoke the refuge and/or flowage easement agreements. Voluntarily relinquish the water rights to the State.

Sheyenne Lake NWR

Proposal and Justification

In 1935, six separate perpetual refuge and flowage easement agreements were signed by private landowners in Sheridan County. On December 21, 1948, these lands became Sheyenne National Wildlife Refuge (figure 23) under the authority of the act of August 14, 1946, a precursor the Fish and Wildlife Coordination Act. An approved acquisition boundary was designated within and around these limited-interest refuge lands totaling 1,273 acres. Because the Service never acquired any of these lands fee title, the purpose of this limited-interest refuge land is contained in the refuge and flowage easement agreements including (a) water conservation, (b) drought relief, (c) a wildlife demonstration unit, and (d) a closed refuge and reservation for migratory birds and other wildlife.

The lands on which the limited-interest refuge is located have been purchased in fee title by the BOR for Garrison Diversion Unit purposes, a large irrigation project. As part of the 1986 Garrison Diversion Reformulation Act, the area surrounding and containing the refuge became known as the Lonetree Wildlife Management Area. NDGF currently manages the area under an agreement with BOR.

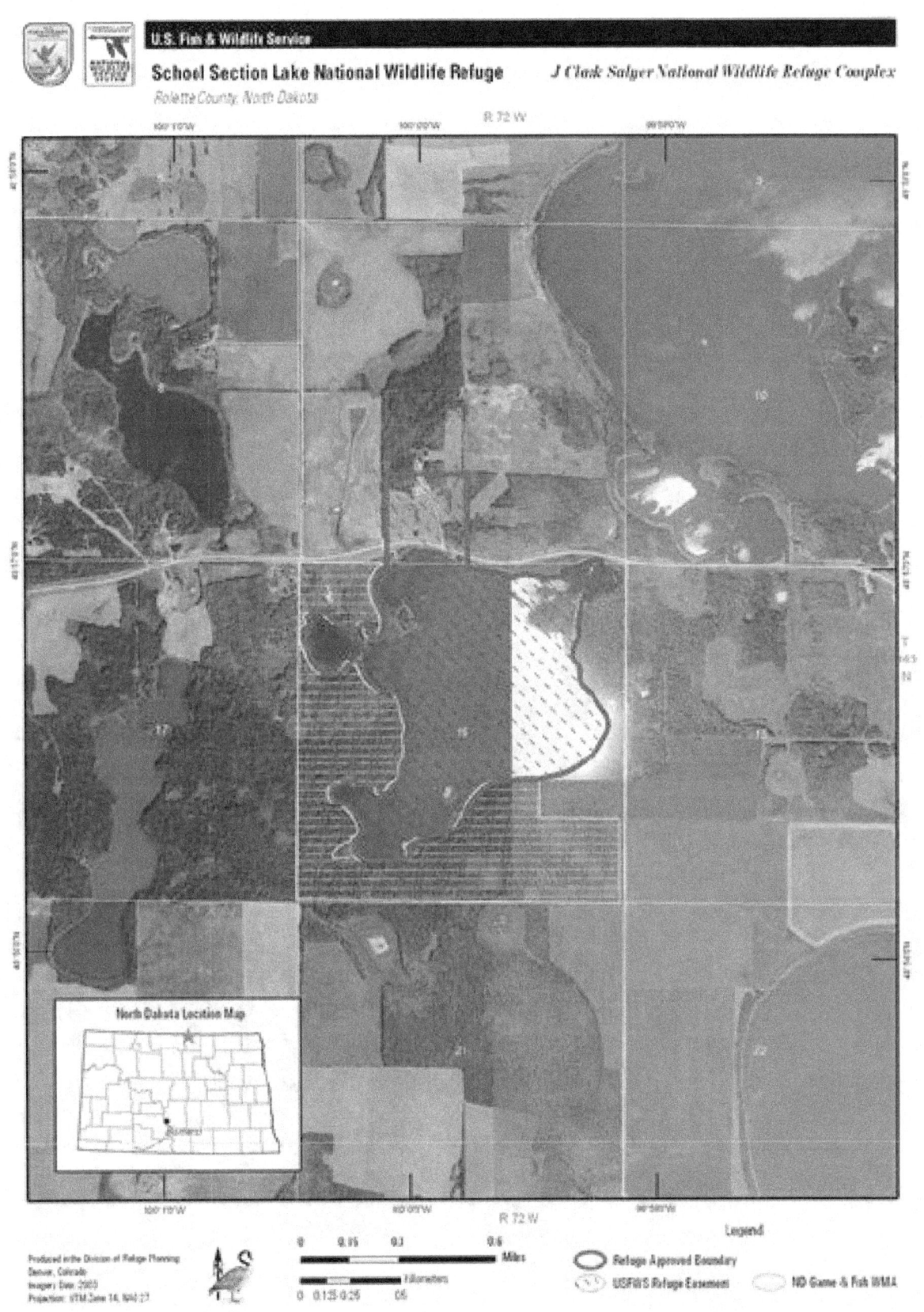

Figure 22. School Section Lake NWR

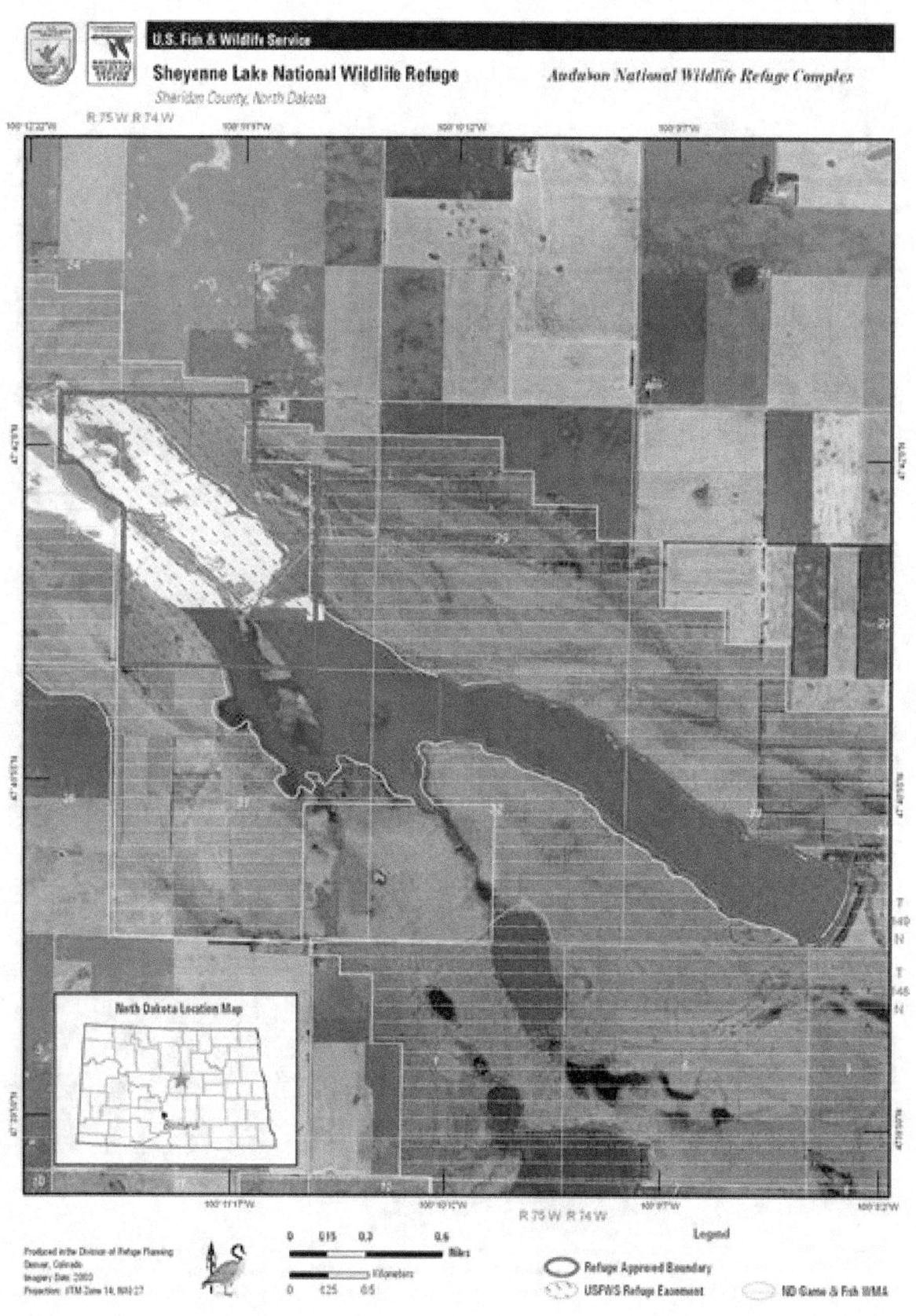

Figure 23. Sheyenne Lake NWR

The refuge contains both Sheyenne and Coal Mine lakes, which are the principle water areas on the refuge. These lakes provide breeding and migration habitat for waterfowl and other waterbirds. A small amount of uplands surround Sheyenne Lake within the refuge boundary. The NDGF currently manages all lands and water as quality wildlife habitat for migratory birds and other wildlife. Because the wildlife values are being effectively protected and managed by the BOR and the NDGF by order of the 1986 Garrison Diversion Reformulation Act, there is no need for continuing the Service's interest in the agreements or the refuge status.

Recommendation: Divest the limited-interest refuge and revoke the refuge and flowage easement agreements, transferring management and voluntarily relinquishing the water rights to BOR or the State.

Once this CCP is approved, the managing stations would work with the Division of Realty and Land Protection Planning to prepare a combined Program proposal to divest these refuges. As a courtesy, this proposal would be submitted to the Migratory Bird Conservation Commission for concurrence and then submitted for congressional approval. This process could take some time as final divestiture will take an act of Congress.

6.3 Goals, Objectives, and Strategies

The following goals, objectives, and strategies outline the actions needed to achieve the Program vision for the refuges that are not being proposed for divestiture.

The following objectives and strategies address the remaining 33 refuges not proposed for divestiture. The Service will not implement any of the following actions, outside the authority of the limited-interest refuge agreement (see section 2.3), without the cooperation of willing landowners.

Wetland Habitat

Goal: Maintain and manage natural and created wetlands within the approved acquisition boundary to provide habitat for international populations of waterfowl and other migratory birds along with other wetland-dependent wildlife.

Objective 1: Work with the Service's Division of Engineering to evaluate the safety and integrity of all water management facilities; thereafter, annually manage water levels, protecting the Service's water right while working cooperatively with willing landowners to reduce negative impacts from upland uses to ensure productive wetland habitat for wetland-dependant migratory birds.

Completion Year: 2020

Rationale: The structures that impound and control water bodies on the limited-interest refuges were built in the 1930s and 1940s. Some have been replaced or updated, while many others have been altered, removed, or are in disrepair and not fully functioning. Most of the impoundments have not been historically managed for maximum wetland habitat production, primarily due to a lack of staff, funding, and management capability to implement any water level management programs. Many areas have been kept at higher than desirable water levels for many years and several have become popular fishing and boating areas. This was not the intent of the Program as evidenced by the installation of the water level management structures and the agreements. Restoration of the management capability, supported by the necessary staff and funding, is essential to provide habitat to wetland-dependent migratory birds.

Strategies:

Priority 1 (initiate year 1 and thereafter)

1) Refuge staff will work with the Division of Engineering to plan and conduct annual safety and maintenance inspections of water management structures until all have been inspected and maintenance needs have been identified.

2) Install water elevation gauges on all impoundments that have the capability to manage water levels and record levels in the

spring and late summer/early fall during the migration periods.

3) Identify and protect the Service's water rights (see table 10.)

Priority 2

1) Implement any necessary maintenance, repair and replacement to maximize management capabilities. Schedule projects based on safety needs and the habitat protection priorities established by each managing station.

2) Use existing and updated water control structures to create optimum and stable wetland conditions during the nesting and migration seasons of wetland-dependent birds.

Priority 3

1) Develop standard protocol using GIS technologies for monitoring migratory bird response to management actions and make adjustments to maximize production, natural diversity, and survival.

Objective 2: Restore and protect over 2,000 seasonal, temporary, and semi-permanent wetlands, totaling nearly 2,500 acres, that exist within the approved refuge boundaries.

Completion Year: 2020

Rationale: The Service's definition of wetlands states that, "Wetlands are land transitional between terrestrial and aquatic systems where the water table is usually at or near the surface or the land is covered by shallow water" (Cowardin et al. 1979). Wetlands are the link between land and water and serve not only as storage areas for water, preventing flooding, but also absorb excess nutrients, sediments, and other pollutants before they reach rivers, lakes, and other waterbodies. Nearly half of all wildlife species use wetlands at some point in their lives. Many of the U.S. breeding bird populations—including ducks, geese, hawks, wading birds, and songbirds— feed, nest, and raise their young in wetlands. Nevertheless, the U.S. continues to lose over 60,000 acres of wetlands every year (U.S. Environmental Protection Agency 2004).

According to data provided by HAPET, almost 2,500 acres of natural wetlands occur within the boundaries of the limited-interest refuges. Currently, the Service has little ability to manage or protect wetlands for wildlife, particularly for waterfowl and other migratory birds. The Service will need to work with willing landowners to provide additional compensation for critical protection.

Strategies:

Priority 1

1) Provide information on available compensated programs to limited-interest refuge landowners owning lands within priority wetland habitat zones in order to determine their interest in receiving additional compensation for protecting natural wetlands.

2) Each managing station will use HAPET data and other available information to develop a wetland habitat protection priority list for the limited-interest refuges. This list should be reviewed every 10 years, ensuring that the most critical habitat protection needs identified in both regional and national plans (including the North American Waterfowl Management Plan, Shorebird Conservation Plan and others) are being adequately addressed.

Priority 2

1) Using the following programs and funding sources, work with willing landowners and partners to ensure the identified wetlands are restored and protected:

- Acquire wetland easements on natural wetlands in priority areas/counties.
- Refuge Inholding Fund.

Service staff inspects a structure at Sheyenne Lake NWR.

- Prioritize fee acquisition of limited-interest refuges and compete for funding from the Refuge Inholding Fund. To compete for funding from this account, a copy of a signed option to purchase the property must be submitted with the request. The Washington Division of Realty limits funding from this account to tracts of $250,000 or less.

- Migratory Bird Conservation Funds
  - Use of Migratory Bird Conservation Funds would require lands to be managed as WPAs. To spend these funds to acquire land, the Service would need the approval of the Governor and the Migratory Bird Conservation Commission.

- Land and Water Conservation Fund Project
  - Limited-interest refuge lands within the approved acquisition boundary, as identified in the establishing authority, can be purchased from willing landowners using Land and Water Conservation Funds.

Upland Habitat

Goal: Establish a land protection program within the approved acquisition boundary to maintain, restore, and enhance uplands to provide habitat for international populations of waterfowl, other migratory birds, and other wildlife.

Objective 1: Provide opportunity and incentives to all willing landowners to implement upland conservation measures, in particular for native prairie protection, to maintain, enhance, and preserve migratory bird breeding and nesting habitat while reducing negative impacts to the adjacent wetlands, rivers, lakes, and impoundments.

Completion Year: 2020

Rationale: Except for hunting, the Service does not control activities that occur in upland areas. Construction, farming, grazing, economic developments, have occurred on many of the refuges before and since they were established. The water feature of these refuges have made them attractive for residential and recreational development and for economic endeavors such

Appert Lake NWR

Paul Van Ningen/USFWS

as farming, livestock rearing, fertilizer plants, and bait shops. Varying degrees of negative impacts from these activities include a loss of wildlife habitat and an increase in disturbance. Other upland areas remain intact, including large areas of native prairie; however, nothing protects this prairie habitat from plowing or other impacts except for the economic value the land has for grazing and haying. There is an urgent need to work with willing landowners to protect upland habitat from further impacts, particularly lands with intact native prairie habitat. Compensation would be provided and habitat would be restored for the use of migratory birds, waterfowl, and grassland birds. Resident wildlife also would benefit.

Strategies

Priority 1

1) Contact all refuge landowners to provide information on upland habitat enhancement opportunities through the Service Partners Program, NDGF, USDA, and other Program possibilities. Continue to update landowners on program options through the annual newsletter.

2) Each managing station will utilize HAPET data and other available information to develop an upland habitat protection priority list for the limited-interest refuges. This list will be reviewed every 10 years to incorporate any new information, ensuring that the most critical habitat protection needs continue to be addressed. Highest priority will be given to those lands containing native prairie habitat.

3) Work through the Service's Partners for Wildlife Program to offer landowners incentives for restoring and protecting upland habitat for wildlife.

4) Work cooperatively with the USDA to provide information to landowners on BMPs for farming and grazing and other available conservation programs.

Priority 2

1) In cooperation with willing refuge landowners, develop and implement a conservation limited-interest refuge strategy to limit development within the refuge boundary and adjacent zone of influence.

Priority 3

1) Annually evaluate refuge uplands and record opportunities for habitat restoration, enhancement, creation or preservation.

2) Determine which landowners would like their lands evaluated for additional compensation and protection and pursue one of the following methods and/or funding sources based on the landowner's desires and the level of protection needed:

- Acquire grassland easements on upland areas, giving highest priority to lands supporting native prairie habitat.
- Refuge Inholding Fund
  - Prioritize fee acquisition of limited-interest refuges and compete for funding from the Refuge Inholding Fund. To compete for funding from this account, a copy of a signed option to purchase the property must be submitted with the request. The Washington Division of Realty limits funding from this account to tracts of $250,000 or less.

- Migratory Bird Conservation Funds
  - Use of Migratory Bird Conservation Funds would that lands be managed as WPAs. To spend these funds to acquire land, the Service would need the approval of the Governor and the Migratory Bird Conservation Commission.

- Land and Water Conservation Fund Project
  - Limited-interest refuge lands within the approved acquisition boundary, as identified in the establishing authority, can be purchased from willing landowners using Land and Water Conservation Funds.

Priority 4

1) Using GIS technologies, annually monitor the effects of management actions and modify the Program as needed to provide habitat for nesting waterfowl and other migratory birds.

Partnerships

Goal: Foster landowner, community, and regional partnerships to assist in achieving the Program vision while ensuring that 100 percent of all partners gain a greater understanding of the management and resources of these limited-interest refuges.

Objective 1: Landowners would be given the opportunity to participate as partners in managing their respective limited-interest refuge within the context of the refuge and/or flowage easement agreement.

Completion Year: 2007

Rationale: Although the limited-interest refuges are national wildlife refuges, over 98 percent of the lands (44,285 acres) remain in private ownership. The Service owns the water rights (excluding Lake Otis) and can manage water levels on impoundments for migratory birds. The Service also can regulate public uses, including hunting, trapping, and fishing.

Control of uplands and naturally occurring wetlands remains with the landowners. Nevertheless, there has never been a structured program where landowners had a regular avenue to provide feedback or gain information on this Program. Landowners must be kept informed and given opportunities to participate in this Program if the limited-interest refuges are to have any future value for wildlife.

Strategies:

Priority 1

1) Maintain a mailing list and legal descriptions for each landowner, updating it at least annually (county tax assessor offices can provide the most up-to-date ownership information).

2) Contact each landowner prior to implementing a management practice that may have the potential to affect property or adjacent lands.

3) Each refuge headquarters will contact its respective refuge landowners annually through an informational newsletter that includes Program highlights and information on compensation programs available to landowners to further protect and enhance their refuges. A postage-paid comment form will be included with each newsletter to receive any feedback from the landowners.

Priority 2

1) Provide landowners a wildlife observation reporting form in the annual newsletter to record unusual observations of wildlife on their property or other areas of the refuge. Solicit this observation information from willing landowners on a bi-annual basis and highlight unique sightings in the annual newsletter.

Objective 2: Identify and coordinate with potential partners to achieve common goals that enhance and support the North Dakota Limited-interest Program.

Rationale: There is a great potential and need to compensate the limited-interest refuge landowners willing to provide the necessary protections so that these refuge resources will remain protected and intact. It will be essential that all potential partners are informed and engaged in this opportunity to further protect and fulfill the intent of the Program.

Completion Year: 2010

Strategies:

Priority 1

1) Coordinate with all limited-interest refuge managers to develop a list of potential national and regional partners. Prepare an informational packet on the Program including a history of the Program and the need and opportunities for protection; provide this packet to all potential partners.

2) Invite all interested landowners to meet with potential partners and learn about any programs available for compensating landowners for added wildlife habitat protections.

Objective: On the current 607 NWR fee-title acres (and any future fee-title lands), utilize fire management to protect life, property, and other resources from wildfire while utilizing an ecosystem management approach to restore wildlife habitat.

Priority 1

1) Work cooperatively with affected landowners when planning any prescribed fire operations.

2) Include all NWR fee-title lands within the limited-interest refuges in any managing station fire management plans.

Visitor Services

Goal: Where compatible, and in cooperation with willing landowners, allow public fishing, hunting, trapping, and other high quality wildlife-dependent recreation opportunities that foster an appreciation and understanding of the management and resources of the Program and the System.

Objective 1: Where compatible and in cooperation with willing landowners, the Service's fisheries management program, and the NDGF, evaluate each refuge for the potential to develop consumptive public use programs (hunting, sport fishing, and trapping) that will not negatively impact migratory birds.

Completion Year: 2013

Ring-necked Pheasant
Bob Savannah/USFWS

Rationale: The Service acquired the right to control fishing, trapping, and hunting on all limited-interest refuges. Since the refuges were established in the 1930s and 1940s, all have been open to trapping, while only a few have been officially opened to hunting and fishing. When they were established, market hunting was rampant and there was a need for sanctuaries for migratory birds and other wildlife. Today, hunting, trapping, and fishing uses are strictly regulated and considered by many to be a legitimate, traditional recreational use of renewable natural resources. Healthy wildlife and fish populations produce harvestable surpluses that are a renewable resource. As practiced on refuges, hunting, trapping and fishing do not pose a threat to the wildlife populations and, in some instances, are actually necessary for sound wildlife management. In particular, trapping of smaller predators is essential to the future survival of waterfowl and other ground nesting birds. These small predators (such as raccoon and skunks) have responded favorably to the fragmented habitats that occur in North Dakota. This fragmentation is caused by development and agriculture. Larger predators, such as wolves and bears, have been extirpated from the landscape due their needs for unbroken large tracts of land. Smaller predators have thrived in this unnatural habitat, expanding their populations, which then feed on ground nesting birds, their eggs and young. This combined with habitat losses has imperiled many populations of ground nesting birds. Man created this situation and it is only man's intervention that can correct it. The most effective means, short of acquiring very large tracts of intact habitats (rarely seen today) is to control these predators at more natural population level. This also benefits the predators themselves and the surrounding communities by reducing disease outbreaks amongst wildlife and domestic animals. It also reduces economic damage caused by these predators such as crop depredation. Trapping supports the purposes for which these refuges were established; protection of migratory birds.

Several landowners asked the Service to address crop damage due to the concentration of white-tailed deer and geese within these protected areas. There were other requests to open these areas for additional recreational opportunities. The decision to permit hunting, trapping and fishing on the limited-interest refuges would be made on a case-by-case basis.

Landowners must be willing to provide access to the public. Once access is granted, the final decision to open a refuge would be based on biological soundness, economic feasibility, effects on other refuge programs, resident landowner and visitor safety, and public demand.

The limited-interest refuges are still in private ownership; if they are to be opened to any visitor services, they must be open to the public. The Service may restrict the number of users and the length of the seasons, but it may not exclude the public from the opportunity to participate.

Strategies:

Priority 1

1) Working with the Service's fisheries management program, develop a partnership with NDGF to develop hunting, fishing, and trapping programs and monitor the results.

2) Meet with willing landowners to discuss the opportunities and need for a consumptive use program and determine how public access will be provided.

3) Provide ice fishing opportunities on refuges where the use is compatible.

4) Ensure the existing permit-only trapping programs focuses efforts on those habitats most suitable for ground nesting birds in order to improve survival rates. Implement the International Association of Fish and Wildlife Agencies recommendations for Best Management Practices for trapping wildlife, when available.

5) Ensure that existing hunting and fishing programs have been determined to be compatible and are open to the general public.

Priority 2

1) Do compatibility determinations on each refuge for every individual use being considered.

2) Use the provisions and procedures outlined in the Code of Federal Regulations, Title 50, part 32 to evaluate expanded hunting and fishing opportunities.

3) Determine the need for any restrictions on hunting, fishing, and trapping such as issuing a limited number of permits, shortened seasons, and closed areas.

Priority 3

1) Annually monitor migratory bird breeding and staging use at each refuge to determine the continued compatibility of fishing, hunting, and trapping.

2) At a minimum, every 5 years, the Service will evaluate the Program with the landowner and the NDGF to determine the continued need for hunting, fishing, and trapping uses.

Objective 2: Where compatible and in cooperation with willing landowners, evaluate each refuge for the potential to develop nonconsumptive wildlife-dependent public use programs (wildlife viewing and photography, environmental education, and interpretation) for the general public to better enjoy and understand the Program.

Completion Year: 2013

Rationale: No organized nonconsumptive activity occurs on the limited-interest refuges. In fact, most of the public is unaware these refuges exist. Most of the refuges have the boundaries posted, but few have entrance signs and none have information stations. The public and several landowners expressed some interest in providing opportunities for wildlife viewing and photography, interpretation and environmental education. On any lands not owned by the Service, the landowners have the right to deny access for nonconsumptive visitor services. Therefore, any development of these programs on private lands will only be with the permission of willing landowners.

Strategies:

Priority 1

1) In cooperation with willing landowners, work with state agencies and other interested partners to develop nonconsumptive wildlife-dependent recreational programs.

Priority 2

1) Use the provisions and procedures outlined in the Code of Federal Regulations, Title 50,

One of the few entrance signs.

Mike Goos/USFWS

part 26, Subpart C, Public Use and Recreation, to evaluate and open the limited-interest refuges to any nonconsumptive visitor services.

2) Do compatibility determinations on each refuge for every nonconsumptive use being considered.

Priority 3 (initiate year 3)

1) Work with willing landowners, area groups, and schools to promote awareness of key refuge resources. Look for opportunities to develop cooperative interpretive and environmental education programs for adults and students while promoting ecotourism opportunities for the general public.

2) Place entrance signs and informational kiosks on refuges that provide these opportunities.

Priority 4 (initiate year 3 and thereafter)

1) Monitor migratory bird breeding and staging use at each refuge to determine the continued compatibility of wildlife viewing, photography, interpretation and environmental education.

Objective 3: Provide for visitor safety and ensure adequate signage on all limited-interest refuges.

Completion Year: 2008

Rationale: Since these refuges were established, there has been some variation in the identification of the refuge boundaries and names of the limited-interest refuges. Most have posted boundaries using the common "blue goose" sign, but few have the traditional entrance sign identifying them as national wildlife refuges. There needs to be some consistency in identifying and posting, based on the public activities that are allowed by the landowners. At a minimum, all of the limited-interest refuge boundaries need to be identified due to their restricted uses, such as hunting and fishing, and refuge purpose, to reduce disturbance to migratory birds.

Strategies:

Priority 1

1) Develop a unique boundary sign for all limited-interest refuges so the public may distinguish these privately owned refuges and their restrictions from a traditional fee-title refuge.

Priority 2 (initiate year 1 and thereafter)

1) Inspect and replace boundary signs as needed on all limited-interest refuges.

Priority 3

1) As new wildlife-dependent recreational activities are established, identify unmet law enforcement and visitor services needs and develop a Refuge Operating Needs System and a Maintenance Management System to ensure a safe, quality experience for refuge visitors.

Administration

Goal: Secure and effectively use funding, staffing, and partnerships to ensure the Program meets its full potential of habitat protection and visitor use.

Objective: Secure funding, staffing and develop partnerships to protect and manage the limited-interest refuges, their resources and values, and achieve all Program objectives.

Rationale: Since the Program was established, no staff and little to no funding has been available to manage the refuges. In the past 70 years, the Service has acquired 7 percent (3,443 acres) of the total acres, 2,828 acres of which were acquired as WPAs. There have been a few attempts to review this Program and determine the resources needed to ensure these areas were adequately managed, enhanced, and protected. Most of these

attempts have been unsuccessful, resulting in a continued altering or loss of wildlife habitat. It is imperative that resources and partnerships are sought to ensure adequate protection and management.

Strategies:

Priority 1

1) Recruit one North Dakota Limited-interest Program Coordinator to facilitate the implementation of this plan.

Priority 2

1) Develop Cooperative Conservation Initiative, Challenge Cost Share, and North American Wetlands Conservation Act grants and other grants with available partners to obtain funding for habitat and other protection work.

2) Incorporate management of limited-interest refuges into annual work plans.

3) Use volunteers to assist with management, maintenance, and visitor use programs.

4) Complete a Refuge Operating Needs System or a Maintenance Management System proposal to request dollars for any projects requiring Service funding.

5) Recruit four seasonal law enforcement officers to ensure visitor safety and enforce established refuge regulations.

6.4 Step-down Management Plans

This strategic CCP will guide the future direction of the Program. Implementation of this CCP will require further strategies detailed in step-down management plans (see table 16).

Most of the limited-interest refuges have been included in the managing stations management plans. Because these refuges are in private ownership, opportunities for management, beyond those described in section 2.3, are limited. This fact makes it difficult to complete many step-down plans until the future of these refuges is more certain. However, a significant part of implementing this CCP will be for each managing station to complete an evaluation and prioritization of their refuges identifying the

Table 16. Limited-interest refuge step-down management plans

Plan/Proposal	Years 1–3	Years 4–6	As Related to Changes in Individual Refuge Status
Limited-interest Refuge Habitat Priority List	X		
Divestiture Proposals	X		
Wildlife Management Plans (may be incorporated in Complex/WMD plans)			
Waterfowl	X		
Shorebirds and Water Birds	X		
Neotropical Migrant/Birds of Concern		X	
Resident Game Species			X
Nongame Species			X
Fisheries		X	
Wildlife Inventory	X		
Integrated Pest Management Plan	X		
Habitat Management Plans (may be incorporated in Complex/WMD plans)			
Moist Soil/Water	X		
Grassland			X
Fire Management Plan			X
Visitor Services Plans			X
Hunting and Trapping			X
Fishing			X
Wildlife Observation and Photography, Environmental Education and Interpretation			X
Sign	X		
Law Enforcement	X		

most imperiled and critical habitat areas. This will assist in ranking future project opportunities.

Step-down plans are primarily for those refuges where the Service will be able to secure additional protections from willing landowners. These step-down plans may continue to be incorporated into Complex or WMD plans, if appropriate.

6.5 Partnership Opportunities

A major objective of this CCP is to establish partnerships with landowners, volunteers, private organizations, and state and federal natural resource agencies. In particular, voluntary participation from limited-interest refuge landowners is essential to the success of this plan. Landowners will be informed of opportunities to participate in compensated habitat protection programs; it will be their option to participate. Opportunities exist near the limited-interest refuges to establish

partnerships with sporting clubs, elementary and secondary schools, and community organizations. A strong partnership already exists between the Service and NDGF. At regional and state levels, partnerships might be established with organizations such as Ducks Unlimited, The Nature Conservancy, Audubon Society, National Wild Turkey Federation, North Dakota Wildlife Federation and Wildlife Societies, and Delta Waterfowl.

6.6 Monitoring and Evaluation

Adaptive management is a flexible approach to long-term management of biotic resources. Adaptive management is directed over time by the results of ongoing monitoring activities and other information. More specifically, adaptive management is a process by which projects are implemented within a framework of scientifically driven experiments to test the predictions and assumptions outlined within a plan (figure 24).

To apply adaptive management, specific survey, inventory, and monitoring protocols will be adopted for the Complex. The habitat management strategies will be systematically evaluated to determine management effects on wildlife populations. This information will be used to refine approaches and determine how effectively the objectives are being accomplished. Evaluations will include HAPET, ecosystem team, and other appropriate partner participation.

If monitoring and evaluation indicate undesirable effects for target and nontarget species or communities, alterations to the management projects will be made. Subsequently, the CCP will be revised.

Specific monitoring and evaluation activities will be described in the step-down management plans (see section 6.4).

6.7 CCP Amendment and Revision

This CCP will be reviewed annually to determine the need for revision. A revision would occur if and when significant information becomes available, such as a change in ecological conditions or significant landowner interest in additional programs. The final CCP would be augmented by detailed step-down management plans to address the completion of specific strategies in support of the Program's goals and objectives. The step-down management plans and revisions to the CCP would be subject to public review and NEPA compliance.

At a minimum, this CCP will be evaluated every 5 years and revised after 15 years.

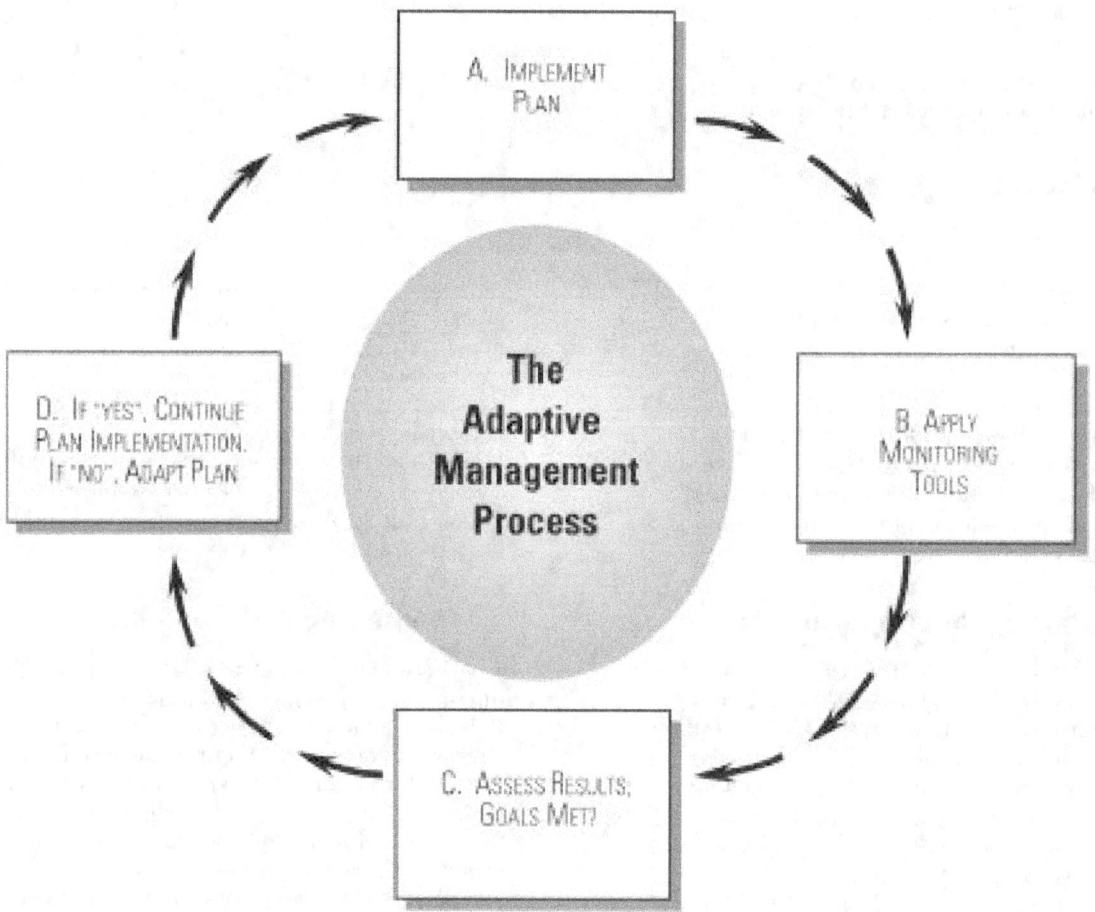

Figure 24. Adaptive Management.

Appendix A. Consultation and Coordination

A planning team (see table A-1) composed of representatives from the six managing stations, various other Service Divisions, and a representative from NDGF was formed to prepare this CCP and EA. Initially, the team focused on identifying the issues and concerns pertinent to the management of the Program. The team met on several occasions and participated in public scoping activities throughout the state. During this period, the team also sought the contributions of experts (table A-2) from various fields of expertise.

Table A-1. Planning team members

Name	Title	Agency
Laura King	Planning Team Leader, Refuge Operations Specialist	U.S. Fish and Wildlife Service
Randy Kreil	Division Chief, Wildlife Division	North Dakota Game and Fish Department
Rod Krey	Refuge Supervisor, ND/SD	U.S. Fish and Wildlife Service
Bob Barrett	Deputy Refuge Supervisor, ND/SD	U.S. Fish and Wildlife Service
Sean Fields	Wildlife Biologist/GIS Specialist	U.S. Fish and Wildlife Service
Lloyd Jones	Refuge Coordinator, North Dakota	U.S. Fish and Wildlife Service
Ron Reynolds	Project Leader, Region 6 HAPET Office	U.S. Fish and Wildlife Service
Stu Wacker	Supervisory Realty Specialist	U.S. Fish and Wildlife Service
Roger Hollevoet	Project Leader, Devils Lake	U.S. Fish and Wildlife Service
Kim Hanson	Project Leader, Arrowwood	U.S. Fish and Wildlife Service
Bob Vanden Berge	Project Leader (retired 1/05), Kulm	U.S. Fish and Wildlife Service
Bob Howard	Project Leader (retired 6/04), J. Clark Salyer	U.S. Fish and Wildlife Service
Tedd Gutzke	Project Leader, J. Clark Salyer	U.S. Fish and Wildlife Service
Mike McEnroe	Project Leader (retired 1/05), Audubon	U.S. Fish and Wildlife Service
Paul Van Ningen	Project Leader, Long Lake	U.S. Fish and Wildlife Service
Lee Albright	Wetland District Manager, J. Clark Salyer	U.S. Fish and Wildlife Service
Dave Azure	Deputy Project Leader, Kulm	U.S. Fish and Wildlife Service
Gary Williams	Deputy Project Leader, Audubon	U.S. Fish and Wildlife Service
Natoma (Tomi) Buskness	Deputy Project Leader, Long Lake	U.S. Fish and Wildlife Service
Jim Alfonso	Deputy Project Leader, Devils Lake	U.S. Fish and Wildlife Service
Mark Vaniman	Deputy Project Leader (transferred 2/04), Arrowwood	U.S. Fish and Wildlife Service
Stacy Adolf-Whipp	Wetland District Manager, Arrowwood	U.S. Fish and Wildlife Service
Stacy Hoehn	Refuge Operations Specialist, Valley City	U.S. Fish and Wildlife Service
Kory Richardson	Wetland District Manager, Valley City	U.S. Fish and Wildlife Service
Mike Goos	Wetland District Manager, Audubon	U.S. Fish and Wildlife Service
Michael (Mick) Erickson	Wetland District Manager, Arrowwood	U.S. Fish and Wildlife Service
Paul Halko	Wetland District Manager, Devils Lake	U.S. Fish and Wildlife Service
Neil Shook	Wetland District Manager, Devils Lake	U.S. Fish and Wildlife Service
Kurt Tompkins	Wetland District Manager, Devils Lake	U.S. Fish and Wildlife Service

Table A-2. Other contributors to the Limited-interest National Wildlife Refuges CCP and their area(s) of expertise

Name	Title	Area of Expertise
Ron Shupe	Deputy Chief of Refuges	Limited-interest refuge history
Harvey Wittmier	Realty Chief	Limited-interest refuge history, realty policies and procedures
Michael Spratt	Planning Division Chief	Planning processes and techniques
Linda Kelly	Chief, Comprehensive Conservation Planning	Planning processes and techniques
Bill Reffault	President, Blue Goose Alliance	Limited-interest refuge history
Margo Zalen	Regional Solicitor, Denver	Legal guidance and opinion
Alan Palisoul	WO Solicitor	Legal guidance and opinion
Betty Adler	Supv. Realty Specialist	Realty history of limited-interest refuges and procedures
James Eaglesome	Paralegal Specialist (Realty)	Legal guidance and opinion
Cheryl Willis	Water Resources Division Chief	Water resources information; water rights
Sandy Hutchcroft	Supv. Information Technology Specialist	Realty database
David Redhorse	Native American Liaison	Native American interests
Jane Fitzgerald	Reference Archivist, Old Military and Civil Records	Historical records related to limited-interest refuges
John Esperance	Chief, Land Protection Planning	Land protection planning guidance
Joyce Welch	GIS Contractor	Limited-interest refuge history and mapping
Rhoda Lewis	Regional Archaeologist	Cultural and archeological resources guidance
Sue Kvas	GIS Specialist, HAPET	GIS and related habitat data, HAPET
Sean Furniss	Refuge Roads Coordinator	Refuge purposes
Deb Parker	Editor, Planning	Editing
Aleta Powers	Natural Resource Specialist	Editing (Contractor)
Connie Young-Dubovsky	Regional NEPA Coordinator	NEPA compliance
Eva Paredes	Facility Management Coordinator	Real property inventory

Public Review of the Draft CCP/EA

The public was given a 60-day period to review the public draft plan. The review period ended December 2, 2005. During the month of October 2005, newsletters summarizing the draft plan and comment forms were sent to over 730 individuals on the mailing list. In addition, over 100 copies of the plan were sent to interested parties. A total of 6 public meetings were held to give the public an opportunity to discuss the public draft of the CCP. These meetings were held in October in the communities of Valley City, McHenry, Devils Lake, Upham, Oakes, and Moffitt, N.D. A presentation was given at each meeting summarizing the draft plan and comments were collected. We had a total of 19 attendees. More than 20 news releases and articles were prepared regarding the draft plan and these public meetings.

The following issues, concerns, and comments are a compilation and summary of those expressed during the draft CCP comment period. Comments were provided by the public, other Federal and State agencies, and individuals concerned about the natural resources of these refuges. The section is organized by topics and presents both the comment and the Service's response. Only those substantive comments that are relative to this planning effort and within the jurisdiction of the Service are addressed and considered.

Public Comments

The refuge staff recognizes and appreciates all input received from the public throughout the planning process. In particular, the feedback, comments, and renewed interactions with the landowners of these refuges has been essential to this planning process. All comments were reviewed by the planning team. In many cases we received similar comments or questions from multiple persons or organizations. These comments have been combined and paraphrased. The following summarizes all substantive comments followed by the Service's response.

Divestiture

Comment 1—The Service should retain all refuges proposed for divestiture and develop agreements with the state and acquire the uplands from the landowners.

Response: Prior to divestiture, the Service will work closely with both the state and landowners to ensure there is not net loss of wildlife habitat (if any) that currently exists on these refuges. The state currently manages three of these refuges as Wildlife Management Areas (WMA) and owns all or most of the lands within two of these refuges. The Service is there in name only. The third refuge was acquired by the Bureau of Reclamation who has an agreement with the state to manage it as a WMA. The remaining three refuges either never had or have lost their wildlife values to the point that they no longer support the goals of the National Wildlife Refuge System. The Service made these determinations based on discussions amongst managers, biologists, and the directorate. The resulting divestiture model used as a tool to examine each refuge in

this project for divestiture has been added in appendix G. By divesting these refuges, any future funding will then be used to enhance and protect those lands and waters that can truly function as refuges as described in the National Wildlife Refuge System Improvement Act.

Comment 2—Concerned about the lack of procedure to consider proposed divestment of refuge lands.

Response: An appendix has been added to the document describing the divestiture decision model developed by the Region and used as part of the process to determine which refuges should be considered for divestiture.

Comment 3—The Service should have taken a more aggressive look at the divestiture issue and considered divesting additional refuges.

Response: The Service used the divestiture model (as described in appendix G) as a tool to determine which refuges should be considered for divestiture. This was the first use of this model and it may be refined in the future. During a divestiture workshop, the information for analyzing these refuges was provided by a team of managers and biologists who currently manage these areas. Based on this information, only six of the 39 refuges met the current criteria for divestiture consideration. The Service recognizes that there has been little attention given to these refuges since they were established. No funding has even been earmarked for management of this program. However, this plan is the most effective tool for elevating issues and requesting funding to properly manage these refuges. There are no guarantees, but it is certain that if this plan had not been completed, the directorate, who makes decisions on budgeting, would remain unaware of the needs to properly managing these refuges.

Hunting and Trapping

Comment 1—A number of comments were received both for and against trapping on these refuges. Those opposed to trapping stated that it was cruel and that the EA failed to adequately justify continuing a trapping program. Those supporting trapping identified it as a valuable wildlife management tool for protecting ground nesting birds and endangered species.

Response: The Service has expanded the sections in the document discussing the benefits of trapping to ground nesting bird survival. Predators (such as raccoons, skunks, and foxes) and habitat loss are the greatest threats to ground nesting birds. Small predators such as those mentioned have responded favorably to the fragmented habitats caused by development and agriculture. Their natural predators, such as wolves and grizzlies, have not. This has created an overabundant, unnatural population of these small predators which are effective hunters of ground nesting birds, in particular waterfowl, eggs, and young birds. Without this intervention, along with other methods, such as electrical fences and exclosures, nesting success would plummet. This would be devastating in this part of the country known as North America's "Duck Factory".

Response: The Service will revisit this issue when the International Association of Fish and Wildlife Agencies completes it's research and develops a list of standard 'Best Management Practices' for trapping on public lands.

Comment 2—A variety of comments were received regarding the Service's proposal to work with willing landowners and the state to determine if any additional hunting opportunities are available. We heard from both those who oppose and support hunting on these refuges.

Response: The National Wildlife Refuge Improvement Act lists hunting as a priority public use on refuges when deemed compatible. It is not certain at this time whether any additional refuges will be opened for hunting. This determination will be made as part of implementation. It will be essential that willing landowners agree to provide access, but this is their decision, not a decision by the Service. Once access is granted, a compatibility determination will be completed for each proposed use. The public will be permitted to see these compatibility determinations. The document emphasizes that no additional public uses will be permitted unless access is granted, the resources are available to manage the use, and the use is deemed compatible with the purposes of the refuge, i.e. the use does not negatively impact migratory birds, in particular migrating waterfowl.

Comment 3—A few refuge landowners were concerned about opening their lands to public hunting due to the impacts to migrating waterfowl.

Response: No additional activities, including hunting, will be permitted on any refuge unless it is found compatible with the purposes for which it was established. In the case of the limited-interest refuges, the purpose includes a refuge for migratory birds, particularly waterfowl. If a willing landowner would like to have their lands open to public hunting (for white-tailed deer and certain geese species), the Service will ensure that this use does not impact migrating ducks in the spring and fall. Shortened seasons, permit-only hunting, or limited access are some tools to accomplish this. First and foremost, a landowner must be willing to grant access before the Service will even consider allowing public uses, including hunting. No limited-interest refuge is "automatically" open to any public use unless access is granted by willing landowners and the use is found compatible with the purposes of that refuge.

Fishing
Comment 1—Concerned that fishing on the James River (Dakota NWR) impacts spawning fish in the spring.

Response: The Service Fisheries Division will work closely with the state to ensure areas open to fishing are compatible with the purposes of the refuge while ensuring that the fishery is not negatively impacted and can sustain the use.

Funding and Staffing
Comment 1—It appears that the state coordinator would be essential to implementing this plan, how does the Service propose to get this position and other funding to implement this plan?

Response: Once this plan is approved, the Service will pursue the staff and funding necessary to implement this plan. Although there is no guarantee of funding, submitting this plan has made the decision makers aware of the needs of this program, something that had not been done at such a comprehensive level. If funding does come available, the landowners, and other who wish to remain on the mailing list, will be given this information in the annual newsletter.

Comment 2—The plan should address potential opportunities to examine current allocations of funding and resources a bit further.

Response: In the 70 year history of this program, there has never been any funds specifically earmarked for these refuges. This has lead to disrepair of water management structures and lack of interaction with refuge landowners. This planning process has renewed interest in these refuges and elevated the needs of this program.

Impoundments
Comment 1—There is no discussion on the Service's ability to stop the draining of the impoundments.

Response: The document does state that the Service controls the water level and uses that occur on the impoundments or main body of water over which it holds a water right. This includes the ability to stop any draining of this impoundment if that is not within water level management objectives.

Incompatible Uses
Comment 1—How will the Service communicate to the landowners which uses are compatible with the purposes of these refuges?

Response: This planning process was the first attempt to review both historical records in combination with Solicitor's opinions to pinpoint both the Service's and landowner rights on these refuges. There is a discussion of this in section 2.3 of the document. Since this program began, there have been some inconsistencies in the uses permitted on these refuges. The Service recognized this and ensured this rights determination was made early in the planning process. This is essential to the future of these refuges and for building relationships with the landowners. Any use under the authority of the Service that is proposed for these refuges will have to have a compatibility determination made to determine if it is compatible with the purposes of that refuge. The Service will work with the affected landowners when completing this determination and will take necessary actions to allow or deny a proposed use based on an impact analysis.

Signage
Comment 1—The new boundary sign for these refuges should identify these refuges as private lands and identify the limited uses that may occur within the limited-interest refuge boundary, if any.

Response: The proposed limited-interest boundary sign will provide this information.

Wetland and Grassland Protection
Comment 1—The Service should evaluate any wetlands and grasslands being considered for added protection using the same acquisition criteria used for wetland and native prairie grassland easements elsewhere in North Dakota.

Response: The Service will use both the wetland and grassland easement programs to compensate willing landowners for added protections. Therefore, the current criteria for these programs will be used for evaluating each future proposal.

Comment 2—The Service should work diligently to acquire the necessary upland habitat to prevent further loss of habitat.

Response: The plan includes objectives for the Service to work with willing landowners to provide additional compensation for added protection of upland habitats.

Crop Depredation
Comment 1—There were numerous comments from landowners reiterating that they are losing significant amounts of crops to concentrated populations of geese (in particular snow and Canada's) and white-tailed deer.

Response: This was a frequent comment heard from landowners during the initial scoping process. The Service recognizes that crop depredation is an issue on these refuges. To address this issue, the Service has proposed in the plan to work with willing landowners and the state to open certain refuges to public hunting of certain geese species and white-tailed deer.

Invasive Species
Comment 1—The Service should control the invasive species that occur on the uplands of these limited-interest refuges.

Response: The Service has determined that the easement did not give the government the right to control the uses that occur on the uplands. This means that landowners are able to farm, graze, build homes, etc., on these upland areas. This also means the Service is not responsible for such activities as controlling invasive plants that occur on these uplands. This is the responsibility of the landowners.

Landowner Relations

Comment 1—The Service should work more closely with the landowners and let them know when things are occurring on their respective refuges.

Response: The plan includes a partnership goal and several objectives and strategies for interacting with landowners while keeping them informed about activities and programs that affect their respective refuges. At a minimum, each landowner and other interested parties will receive an annual newsletter updating them on the implementation of this plan and other opportunities for partnerships. The Service will also coordinate with landowners when any projects or enhancements are planned for their respective refuge.

Appendix B. Glossary of Terms

adaptive management—a process in which projects are implemented within a framework of scientifically driven experiments to test predictions and assumptions outlined within the comprehensive conservation plan. The analysis of the outcome of project implementation helps managers determine whether current management should continue as is or whether it should be modified to achieve desired conditions.

alternative—a reasonable way to fix the identified problem or satisfy the stated need (40 CFR 1500.2) [see also *management alternative* below].

approved acquisition boundary—a project boundary which the Director of the Fish and Wildlife Service approves upon completion of the detailed planning and environmental compliance process.

biological integrity—composition, structure, and function at the genetic, organism, and community levels consistent with natural conditions, and the biological processes that shape genomes, organisms, and communities.

biological or natural diversity—the abundance, variety, and genetic constitution of animals and plants in nature. Also referred to as 'biodiversity.'

boreal—describes a region that has a northern temperature climate, with cold winters and warm summers.

breeding habitat—habitat used by migratory birds or other animals during the breeding season.

buffer zone or buffer strip—protective land borders around critical habitats or water bodies that reduce runoff and nonpoint source pollution loading; areas created or sustained to lessen the negative effects of land development on animals and plants and their habitats.

CFR—Code of Federal Regulations.

community—the area or locality in which a group of people resides and shares the same government.

compatibility determination—a compatibility determination is required for a wildlife-dependant recreational use or any other public use of a refuge. A compatible use is one which, in the sound professional judgment of the refuge manager, will not materially interfere with or detract from fulfillment of the Refuge System Mission or refuge purpose(s).

compatible use—an allowed use that will not materially interfere with, or detract from, the purposes for which the unit was established (Service Manual 602 FW 1.4).

comprehensive conservation plan (CCP)—a document that describes the desired future conditions of a refuge or planning unit and provides long-range guidance and management direction to achieve the purposes of the refuge, help fulfill the mission of the System, maintain and, where appropriate, restore the biological integrity, diversity, and environmental health of each refuge and the System, and meet other mandates.

concern—see *issue*.

conservation—the management of natural resources to prevent loss or waste. Management actions may include preservation, recovery, restoration, and enhancement.

cooperative agreement—the legal instrument used when the principal purpose of the transaction is the transfer of money, property, services or anything of value to a recipient in order to accomplish a public purpose authorized by federal statute and substantial involvement between the Service and the recipient is anticipated.

coteau—a hilly upland or a divide between two valleys.

cultural resources—evidence of historic or prehistoric human activity, such as buildings, artifacts, archaeological sites, documents, or oral or written history.

database—a collection of data arranged for ease and speed of analysis and retrieval, usually computerized.

easement—an agreement by which a landowner gives up or sells one of the rights on his/her property.

ecosystem—a biological community together with its environment, functioning as a unit. For administrative purposes, the Service has designated 53 ecosystems covering the United States and its possessions. These ecosystems generally correspond with watershed boundaries and vary in their sizes and ecological complexity.

ecotourism—a type of tourism that maintains and preserves natural resources as a basis for promoting economic growth and development resulting from visitation to an area.

emergent vegetation—a vegetation type common in wetlands dominated by erect, rooted, herbaceous plants.

endangered species—a federally protected species which is in danger of extinction throughout all or a significant portion of its range.

environmental assessment (EA)—a concise public document, prepared in compliance with the National Environmental Policy Act, that briefly discusses the purpose and need for an action, alternatives to such action, and provides sufficient evidence and analysis of impacts to determine whether to prepare an environmental impact statement or finding of no significant impact (40 CFR 1508.9).

environmental education—education aimed at producing a citizenry that is knowledgeable concerning the biophysical environment and its associated problems, aware of how to help solve these problems, and motivated to work toward their solution (Stapp et al. 1969).

environmental health—the composition, structure, and functioning of soil, water, air, and other abiotic features comparable with historic conditions, including the natural abiotic processes that shape the environment.

environmental impact statement (EIS)—a detailed written statement required by section 102(2)(C) of the National Environmental Policy Act, analyzing the environmental impacts of a preferred alternative, adverse effects of the project that cannot be avoided, alternative courses of action, short-term uses of the environment versus the maintenance and enhancement of long-term productivity, and any irreversible and irretrievable commitment of resources (40 CFR 1508.11).

fauna—all the vertebrae or invertebrate animals of an area.

federal land—public land owned by the federal government, including lands such as national forests, national parks and national wildlife refuges.

federally listed species—a species listed under the federal Endangered Species Act of 1973, as amended, either as endangered, threatened or species at risk (formerly candidate species).

fee title—the acquisition of most or all of the rights to a tract of land.

Finding of no significant impact (FONSI)—a document prepared in compliance with the National Environmental Policy Act, supported by an environmental assessment, that briefly presents why a federal action will have no significant effect on the human environment and for which an environmental impact statement, therefore, will not be prepared (40 CFR 1508.13).

forbs—a flowering plant, excluding grasses, sedges, and rushes, that does not have a woody stem and dies back to the ground at the end of the growing season.

forested land—land dominated by trees. For the purposes of the impacts analysis in this document, all forested land was assumed to have the potential to be occasionally harvested, and forested land owned by timber companies was assumed to be harvested on a more intensive, regular schedule.

geographic information system (GIS)—a computerized system used to compile, store, analyze and display geographically referenced information. Can be used to overlay information layers containing the distributions of a variety of biological and physical features.

goal—descriptive, open-ended, and often broad statement of desired future conditions that conveys a purpose but does not define measurable units.

habitat—the place where a particular type of plant or animal lives. An organism's habitat must provide all of the basic requirements for life and should be free of harmful contaminants.

habitat conservation—the protection of an animal or plant's habitat to ensure that the use of that habitat by the animal or plant is not altered or reduced.

inholding—privately owned land inside the boundary of a national wildlife refuge.

integrated pest management (IPM)—sustainable approach to managing pests by combining biological, cultural, physical, and chemical tools in a way that minimizes economic, health, and environmental risks.

invasive species—nonnative species which have been introduced into an ecosystem, and, because of their aggressive growth habits and lack of natural predators, displace native species.

issue—any unsettled matter that requires a management decision; e.g., a Service initiative, an opportunity, a management problem, a threat to the resources of the unit, a conflict in uses, a public concerns, or the presence of an undesirable resource condition. Issues should be documented, described, and analyzed in the CCP even if resolution cannot be accomplished during the planning process (Service Manual 602 FW 1.4). See also: *key issue*.

limited-interest refuge landowner—a landowner who owns property that is covered by a refuge and/or flowage easement that is located within the approved acquisition boundary of a limited-interest national wildlife refuge.

lacustrine—of, relating to, formed in, living in, or growing in lakes.

local agencies—generally referring to municipal governments, regional planning commissions or conservation groups.

long-term protection—mechanisms such as fee-title acquisition, conservation easements, or binding agreements with landowners that ensure land use and land management practices

will remain compatible with maintenance of the species population at the site.

main body of water—an impoundment, lake or river that occurs within the refuge boundary.

management alternative—a set of objectives and the strategies needed to accomplish each objective (Service Manual 602 FW 1.4).

management concern—see *issue*.

management opportunity—see *issue*.

management plan—a plan that guides future land management practices on a tract of land. In the context of this environmental impact statement, management plans would be designed to produce additional wildlife habitat along with the primary products, such as timber or agricultural crops. See *cooperative agreement*.

migratory—the seasonal movement from one area to another and back.

migratory game birds—birds regulated under the Migratory Bird Treaty Act and state laws, that are legally hunted, includes ducks, geese, woodcock, rails.

monitoring—the process of collecting information to track changes of selected parameters over time.

moraine—a mass of earth and rock debris carried by an advancing glacier and left at its front and side edges as it retreats.

National Environmental Policy Act of 1969 (NEPA)—requires all agencies, including the Service, to examine the environmental impacts of their actions, incorporate environmental information, and use public participation in the planning and implementation of all actions. Federal agencies must integrate NEPA with other planning requirements, and prepare appropriate NEPA documents to facilitate better environmental decision making (from 40 CFR 1500).

national wildlife refuge (refuge)—a designated area of land, water, or an interest in land or water within the System, but does not include Coordination Areas.ʼ Find a complete listing of all units of the System in the current

Annual Report of Lands Under Control of the U.S. Fish and Wildlife Service.

National Wildlife Refuge System (System)—all lands and waters and interests therein administered by the Service as wildlife refuges, wildlife ranges, wildlife management areas, WPAs, and other areas for the protection and conservation of fish and wildlife, including those that are threatened with extinction.

National Wildlife Refuge System Mission (mission)— "The mission of the System is to administer a national network of lands and waters for the conservation, management and, where appropriate, restoration of the fish, wildlife and plant resources and their habitats within the United States for the benefit of present and future generations of Americans."

native plant—a plant that has grown in the region since the last glaciation and occurred before European settlement.

native species—species that normally live and thrive in a particular ecosystem.

Neotropical migratory bird—a bird species that breeds north of the United States/Mexican border and winters primarily south of that border.

nonconsumptive, wildlife-oriented recreation—photographing or observing plants, fish and other wildlife.

notice of intent (NOI)—a notice that an environmental impact statement will be prepared and considered (40 CFR 1508.22). Published in the Federal Register.

objective—a concise statement of what we want to achieve, how much we want to achieve, when and where we want to achieve it, and who is responsible for the work. Objectives derive from goals and provide the basis for determining strategies, monitoring refuge accomplishments, and evaluating the success of strategies. Make objectives attainable, time-specific, and measurable.

Partners for Wildlife Program—a voluntary habitat restoration program undertaken by the Fish and Wildlife Service in cooperation with other governmental agencies, public and private organizations, and private landowners to improve and protect fish and wildlife habitat on private lands while leaving the land in private ownership.

partnership—a contract or agreement entered into by two or more individuals, groups of individuals, organizations or agencies in which each agrees to furnish a part of the capital or some in-kind service, i.e., labor, for a mutually beneficial enterprise.

phenological—periodic biological phenomena the are correlated with climatic conditions.

planning area—a planning area may include lands outside existing planning unit boundaries that are being studied for inclusion in the unit and/or partnership planning efforts. It may also include watersheds or ecosystems that affect the planning area.

planning team—a planning team prepares the comprehensive conservation plan. Planning teams are interdisciplinary in membership and function. A team generally consists of a planning team leader, refuge manager and staff biologist; staff specialists or other representatives of Service programs, ecosystems or regional offices; and state partnering wildlife agencies as appropriate.

Preferred Alternative—the alternative that is preferred by the Service and that will become the management direction in the final document.

priority public uses—see wildlife-dependant recreational uses.

private land—land that is owned by a private individual, group of individuals, or non-governmental organization.

private landowner—any individual, group of individuals or nongovernmental organization that owns land.

private organization—any nongovernmental organization.

proglacial—landforms and deposits just beyond the margin of glacial ice.

proposed action—activities for which an environmental assessment is being written; the alternative containing the actions and strategies recommended by the planning team.

The proposed action is, for all practical purposes, the draft CCP for the refuge.

protection—mechanisms such as fee-title acquisition, conservation easements, or binding agreements with landowners that ensure land use and land management practices will remain compatible with maintenance of the species population at the site.

public—individuals, organizations, and groups; officials of federal, state, and local government agencies; Indian tribes; and foreign nations. It may include anyone outside the core planning team. It includes those who may or may not have indicated an interest in the Service issues and those who do or do not realize that Service decisions may affect them.

public involvement—a process that offers impacted and interested individuals and organizations an opportunity to become informed about, and to express their opinions on Service actions and policies. In the process, these views are studied thoroughly and thoughtful consideration of public views is given in shaping decisions for refuge management.

public land—land that is owned by the local, state, or federal government.

purpose of the refuge—the purpose of the refuge is specified in or derived from the law, proclamation, executive order, agreement, public land order, donation document, or administrative memorandum establishing, authorizing, or expanding a refuge and refuge unit.

refuge goals—descriptive, open-ended and often broad statements of desired future conditions that convey a purpose but do not define measurable units (Writing Refuge Management Goals and Objectives: A Handbook).

refuge lands—those lands in which the Service holds full interest in fee title, or partial interest such as limited-interest refuges.

Refuge Operating Needs System—the Refuge Operating Needs System is a national database, which contains the unfunded operational needs of each refuge. We include projects required to implement approved plans, and meet goals, objectives, and legal mandates.

refuge purposes—the purposes specified in or derived from the law, proclamation, executive order, agreement, public land order, donation document, or administrative memorandum establishing, authorizing, or expanding a refuge, a refuge unit, or refuge subunit, and any subsequent modification of the original establishing authority for additional conservation purposes (Service Manual 602 FW 1.4).

restoration—the artificial manipulation of a habitat to restore it to something close to its natural state.

runoff—water from rain, melted snow, or agricultural or landscape irrigation that flows over the land surface into a water body.

Service presence—the existence of the Service through its programs and facilities which it directs or shares with other organizations; the public awareness of the Service as a sole or cooperative provider of programs and facilities.

species of concern—species present in the watershed for whom the refuge has a special management interest. The following criteria were used to identify a species of concern:

1. Federally listed as threatened or endangered;
2. Migratory bird, especially declining species, Neotropical migrants, colonial waterbirds, shorebirds, or waterfowl;
3. Marine mammal;
4. Sea turtle;
5. Interjurisdictional fish;
6. State-listed as threatened, endangered, or special concern.

state land—public land owned by a state such as state parks or state wildlife management areas.

step-down management plans—step-down management plans describe management strategies and implementation schedules. Step-down management plans are a series of plans dealing with specific management subjects (e.g., croplands, wilderness, and fire) (Service Manual 602 FW 1.4).

strategy—a specific action, tool, technique, or combination of actions, tools, and techniques used to meet unit objectives.

substantive issue—an issue meeting the following three criteria:

- Falls within the jurisdiction of the Service;
- Can be addressed by a reasonable range of alternatives;
- Influences the outcome of the project.

surficial—relating to or occurring on the surface.

threatened species—a federally protected species that is likely to become an endangered species within the foreseeable future throughout all or a significant portion of its range.

trust resource—one that through law or administrative act is held in trust for the people by the government. A federal trust resource is one for which trust responsibility is given in part to the federal government through federal legislation or administrative act. Generally, federal trust resources are those considered to be of national or international importance no matter where they occur, such as endangered species and species such as migratory birds and fish that regularly move across state lines. In addition to species, trust resources include cultural resources protected through federal historic preservation laws, nationally important and threatened habitats, notably wetlands, navigable waters, and public lands such as state parks and national wildlife refuges.

upland—dry ground; other than wetlands.

U.S. Fish and Wildlife Service Mission—our mission is to work with others to "conserve, protect, and enhance fish and wildlife, and their habitat for the continuing benefit of the American people."

vision statement—concise statement of what the unit could be in the next 10 to 15 years

watchable wildlife—all wildlife is watchable. A watchable wildlife program is a strategy to help maintain viable populations of all native fish and wildlife species by building an effective, well-informed constituency for conservation. Watchable wildlife programs are tools by which wildlife conservation goals can be met while at the same time fulfilling public

demand for wildlife recreational activities (other than sport hunting, trapping or sport fishing).

watershed—the geographic area within which water drains into a particular river, stream or body of water. A watershed includes both the land and the body of water into which the land drains.

wetlands—The U.S. Fish and Wildlife Service's definition of wetlands states that "Wetlands are lands transitional between terrestrial and aquatic systems where the water table is usually at or near the surface or the land is covered by shallow water" (Cowardin et al. 1979).

wilderness—The legal definition is found in the Wilderness Act of 1964 Section 2c (P.L. 88-577): "A wilderness, in contrast with those areas where man and his own works dominate the landscape, is hereby recognized as an area where the earth and its community of life are untrammeled by man, where man himself is a visitor who does not remain." This legal definition places wilderness on the "untrammeled" or "primeval" end of the environmental modification spectrum. Wilderness is roadless lands, legally classified as component areas of the National Wilderness Preservation System, and managed so as to protect its qualities of naturalness, solitude and opportunity for primitive types of recreation (Hendee 1990).

wildlife-dependent recreational use—a use of a refuge involving hunting, fishing, wildlife observation and photography, or environmental education and interpretation. These are the six priority public uses of the System as established in the National Wildlife Refuge System Administration Act, as amended. Wildlife-dependent recreational uses, other than the six priority public uses, are those that depend on the presence of wildlife. We also will consider these other uses in the preparation of refuge CCPs, however, the six priority public uses always will take precedence.

wildlife management—the practice of manipulating wildlife populations, either directly through regulating the numbers, ages, and sex ratios harvested, or indirectly by providing favorable habitat conditions and alleviating limiting factors.

Appendix C. Decision Documents

Environmental Action Statement

U.S. Fish and Wildlife Service, Region 6
Lakewood, Colorado

Within the spirit and intent of the Council on Environmental Quality's regulations for implementing the National Environmental Policy Act and other statutes, orders, and policies that protect fish and wildlife resources, I have established the following administrative record.

I have determined that the action of implementing the *Comprehensive Conservation Plan for the North Dakota Limited-interest National Wildlife Refuges* is found not to have significant environmental effects, as determined by the attached Finding of No Significant Impact and the environmental assessment as found with the draft comprehensive conservation plan.

_____ 4/14/06
J. Mitch King   Date
Regional Director
U.S. Fish and Wildlife Service, Region 6
Lakewood, CO

_____ 4/12/06
Richard A. Coleman, Ph.D.   Date
Assistant Regional Director, NWRS
U.S. Fish and Wildlife Service, Region 6
Lakewood, CO

_____ 4/12/06
Rod Krey   Date
Refuge Program Supervisor (ND, SD)
U.S. Fish and Wildlife Service, Region 6
Lakewood, CO

_____ 4/6/06
Kim Hanson   Date
Project Leader
Arrowwood National Wildlife Refuge Complex
Pingree, ND

_____ 4/6/06
Lloyd Jones   Date
Project Leader
Audubon National Wildlife Refuge Complex
Coleharbor, ND

_____ 4/11/06
Roger Hollevoet   Date
Project Leader
Devils Lake Wetland Management District
Devils Lake, ND

_____ 4/6/06
Tedd Gutzke   Date
Project Leader
J. Clark Salyer National Wildlife Refuge Complex
Upham, ND

_____ 4/6/06
Mick Erickson   Date
Project Leader
Kulm Wetland Management District
Kulm, ND

_____ 4/6/06
Paul Van Ningen   Date
Project Leader
Long Lake National Wildlife Refuge Complex
Moffit, ND

Finding of No Significant Impact

U.S. Fish and Wildlife Service, Region 6
Lakewood, Colorado

Two management alternatives for the 39 North Dakota limited-interest national wildlife refuges' programmatic comprehensive conservation plan were assessed as to their effectiveness in achieving the refuges' purposes and their impact on the human environment. Alternative A (the no-action alternative) would continue current management, which has been very minimal, of these refuges. Alternative B ("Enhance the Program," the proposed action) first proposes to consider for divestiture six refuges, which have no potential to fully function as part of the National Wildlife Refuge System. The remaining 33 refuges would be managed in cooperation with willing landowners, the state, and other partners, to (1) evaluate and prioritize habitats for added protection, (2) improve relations and sharing of information with refuge landowners, (3) protect the Service's rights acquired through the easement agreement, and (4) work with willing landowners and the state to determine if additional public use activities such as hunting, fishing, environmental education are feasible on some or all of these refuges. Based on this assessment and comments received, I have selected alternative B for implementation.

The preferred alternative (alternative B) was selected because it best meets the purposes for which these refuges were established and is preferable to the no-action alternative in light of physical, biological, economic, and social factors.

I find that the preferred alternative is not a major federal action that would significantly affect the quality of the human environment within the meaning of Section 102(2)(C) of the National Environmental Policy Act of 1969. Accordingly, the preparation of an environmental impact statement on the proposed action is not required.

The following is a summary of anticipated environmental effects from implementation of the preferred alternative:

— The preferred alternative will not adversely impact endangered or threatened species or their habitat.
— The preferred alternative will not adversely impact archaeological or historical resources.
— The preferred alternative will not adversely impact wetlands nor does the plan call for structures that could be damaged by or that would significantly influence the movement of floodwater.
— The preferred alternative will not have a disproportionately high or adverse human health or environmental effect on minority or low-income populations.
— The State of North Dakota has been notified and given the opportunity to review the comprehensive conservation plan and associated environmental assessment.

_____   4/14/06
J. Mitch King   Date
Regional Director
U.S. Fish and Wildlife Service, Region 6
Lakewood, CO

Appendix D. Key Legislation and Policies

Americans With Disabilities Act (1992): Prohibits discrimination in public accommodations and services.

Antiquities Act (16 U.S.C. 431–433): The act of June 8, 1906, (34 Stat. 225) authorizes the President to designate as National Monuments objects or areas of historic or scientific interest on lands owned or controlled by the United States. The act required that a permit be obtained for examination of ruins, excavation of archaeological sites and the gathering of objects of antiquity on lands under the jurisdiction of the Secretaries of Interior, Agriculture, and Army, and provided penalties for violations.

Archeological and Historic Preservation Act (16 U.S.C. 469–469c): Public Law 86-523, approved June 27, 1960, (74 Stat. 220) as amended by Public Law 93-291, approved May 24, 1974, (88 Stat. 174) to carry out the policy established by the Historic Sites Act (see below), directed federal agencies to notify the Secretary of the Interior whenever they find a federal or federally assisted, licensed or permitted project may cause loss or destruction of significant scientific, prehistoric or archaeologic data. The act authorizes use of appropriated, donated and/or transferred funds for the recovery, protection and preservation of such data.

Archaeological Resources Protection Act (16 U.S.C. 470aa–470ll): Public Law 96-95, approved October 31, 1979, (93 Stat. 721): Largely supplants the resource protection provisions of the Antiquities Act for archaeological items.

This act establishes detailed requirements for issuance of permits for any excavation for or removal of archaeological resources from federal or Indian lands. It also establishes civil and criminal penalties for the unauthorized excavation, removal, or damage of any such resources; for any trafficking in such resources removed from federal or Indian land in violation of any provision of federal law; and for interstate and foreign commerce in such resources acquired, transported, or received in violation of any state or local law.

Public Law 100-588, approved November 3, 1988, (102 Stat. 2983): Lowers the threshold value of artifacts triggering the felony provisions of the act from $5,000 to $500, makes attempting to commit an action prohibited by the act a violation, and requires the land managing agencies to establish public awareness programs regarding the value of archaeological resources to the Nation.

Architectural Barriers Act (1968): Requires federally owned, leased, or funded buildings and facilities to be accessible to persons with disabilities.

Clean Water Act (1977): Requires consultation with the U.S. Army Corps of Engineers for major wetland modifications.

Criminal Code of Provisions of 1940 as amended, (18 U.S.C. 41): States the intent of Congress to protect all wildlife within federal sanctuaries, refuges, fish hatcheries, and breeding grounds. Provides that anyone (except in compliance with rules and regulations promulgated by authority of law) who hunts, traps, or willfully disturbs any such wildlife, or willfully injures, molest, or destroys any property of the United States on such land or water, shall be fined up to $500 or imprisoned for not more than 6 months or both.

Emergency Wetland Resources Act of 1986: Authorizes the purchase of wetlands from Land and Water Conservation Fund moneys, removing a prior prohibition on such acquisitions. The act also requires the Secretary to establish a National Wetlands Priority Conservation Plan, requires the states to include wetlands in their Comprehensive Outdoor Recreation Plans, and transfers to the Migratory Bird Conservation Fund amount equal to import duties on arms and ammunition.

Endangered Species Act of 1973 and recent amendments (16 U.S.C. 1531–1543; 87 Stat. 884) as amended (Establishing legislation.): Provides for conservation of threatened and endangered species of fish, wildlife, and plants by federal action and by encouraging state programs. Specific provisions include:

- The listing and determination of critical habitat for endangered and threatened species and consultation with the Service on any federally funded or licensed project that could affect any of these agencies;
- Prohibition of unauthorized taking, possession, sale, transport, etc..., of endangered species;
- An expanded program of habitat acquisition;
- Establishment of cooperative agreements and grants-in-aid to states that establish and maintain an active, adequate program for endangered and threatened species;
- Assessment of civil and criminal penalties for violating the act or regulations.

Environmental Education Act of 1990 (20 U.S.C. 5501–5510; 104 Stat. 3325): Public Law 101-619, signed November 16, 1990, established the Office of Environmental Education within the Environmental Protection Agency to develop and administer a federal environmental education program.

Responsibilities of the Office include developing and supporting programs to improve understanding of the natural and developed environment, and the relationships between humans and their environment; supporting the dissemination of educational materials; developing and supporting training programs and environmental education seminars; managing a federal grant program; and administering an environmental internship and fellowship program. The Office is required to develop and support environmental programs in consultation with other federal natural resource management agencies, including the Fish and Wildlife Service.

Executive Order 11644, Use of Off-Road Vehicles on Public Lands (1972): Provides policy and procedures for regulating off-road vehicles.

Executive Order 11988, Floodplain Management: This executive order, signed May 24, 1977, prevents federal agencies from contributing to the "adverse impacts associated with occupancy and modification of floodplains" and the "direct or indirect support of floodplain development." In the course of fulfilling their respective authorities, federal agencies "shall take action to reduce the risk of flood loss, to minimize the impact of floods on human safety, health and welfare, and to restore and preserve the natural and beneficial values served by floodplains.

Executive Order 12996, Management and General Public Use of the National Wildlife Refuge System (1996): Defines the mission, purpose, and priority public uses of the National Wildlife Refuge System. It also presents four principles to guide management of the system.

Executive Order 13007, Indian Sacred Sites (1996): Directs federal land management agencies to accommodate access to and ceremonial use of Indian sacred sites by Indian religious practitioners, avoid adversely affecting the physical integrity of such sacred sites, and where appropriate, maintain the confidentiality of sacred sites.

Federal Noxious Weed Act (1990): Requires the use of integrated management systems to control or contain undesirable plant species; and an interdisciplinary approach with the cooperation of other federal and state agencies.

Fish and Wildlife Act of 1956 (70 Stat. 1119; 16 U.S.C. 742a–742J), as amended: Establishes a comprehensive fish and wildlife policy and directs the Secretary of the Interior to provide continuing research; extension and conservation of fish and wildlife resources.

Fish and Wildlife Conservation Act of 1980 (Public Law 96-366, September 29, 1980, 16 U.S.C. 2901–2911, as amended 1986, 1988, 1990 and 1992): Creates a mechanism for federal matching funding of the development of state conservation plans for nongame fish and wildlife. Subsequent amendments to this law require that the Secretary monitor and assess migratory nongame birds, determine the effects of environmental changes and human activities, identify birds likely to be candidates for endangered species listing, and identify conservation actions that would prevent this from being necessary. In 1989, Congress also directed the Secretary to identify lands and waters in the Western Hemisphere, the protection, management or acquisition of which would foster conservation of migratory nongame birds. All of these activities are intended to assist the Secretary in fulfilling the Secretary's responsibilities under the Migratory Bird Treaty Act and the Migratory Bird Conservation Act, and provisions of the Endangered Species Act implementing the Convention on Nature Protection and Wildlife Preservation in the Western Hemisphere.

Fish and Wildlife Improvement Act of 1978: Improves the administration of fish and wildlife programs and amends several earlier laws, including the Refuge Recreation Act, the National Wildlife Refuge Administration Act, and the Fish and Wildlife Act of 1956. It authorizes the Secretary to accept gifts and bequests of real and personal property on behalf of the United States. It also authorizes the use of volunteers on Service projects and appropriations to carry out volunteer programs.

Historic Sites, Buildings and Antiquities Act (16 U.S.C. 461–462, 464–467): The act of August 21, 1935, (49 Stat. 666) popularly known as the Historic Sites Act, as amended by Public Law 89-249, approved October 9, 1965, (79 Stat. 971) declares it a national policy to preserve historic sites and objects of national significance, including those located on refuges. It provides procedures for designation, acquisition, administration and protection of such sites. Among other things, National Historic and Natural Landmarks are designated under authority of this act. As of January 1989, 31 national wildlife refuges contained such sites.

Land and Water Conservation Fund Act (LWCFA) of 1965: Provides funds from leasing bonuses, production royalties and rental revenues for offshore oil, gas, and sulphur extraction to the Bureau of Land Management, the U.S. Forest Service and the U.S. Fish and Wildlife Service, and state and local agencies for purchase of lands for parks, open space, and outdoor recreation.

Migratory Bird Conservation Act of 1929 (16 U.S.C. 715–715d, 715e,715f–715r): Establishes the Migratory Bird Conservation Commission, which consists of the Secretaries of the Interior (chairman), Agriculture, and Transportation, two members from the House of Representatives, and an ex-officio member from the state in which a project is located. The Commission approves acquisition of land and water, or interests therein, and sets the priorities for acquisition of lands by the Secretary for sanctuaries or for other management purposes. Under this act, to acquire lands, or interests therein, the state concerned must consent to such acquisition by legislation. Such legislation has been enacted by most states.

Migratory Bird Conservation Act of 1929 (16 U.S.C. 715-s, 45 Stat. 1222), as amended: Authorizes acquisition, development, and maintenance of migratory bird refuges; cooperation with other agencies, in conservation; and investigations and publications on North American birds. Authorizes payment of 25 percent of net receipts from administration of national wildlife refuges to the country or counties in which such refuges are located.

Migratory Bird Hunting and Conservation Stamp Act of 1934 (16 U.S.C. 718–718h; 48 Stat. 51), as amended: The "Duck Stamp Act," as this March 16, 1934, authority is commonly called, requires each waterfowl hunter 16 years of age or older to possess a valid federal hunting stamp. Receipts from the sale of the stamp are deposited in a special Treasury account known as the Migratory Bird Conservation Fund and are not subject to appropriations.

Migratory Bird Treaty Act of 1918 (16 U.S.C. 703–711; 50 CFR Subchapter B), as amended: Implements treaties with Great Britain (for Canada) and Mexico for protection of migratory birds whose welfare is a federal responsibility. Provides for regulations to control taking, possession, selling, transporting, and importing of migratory birds and provides penalties for violations.

National and Community Service Act of 1990 (42 U.S.C. 12401; 104 Stat. 3127): Public Law 101-610, signed November 16, 1990, authorizes several programs to engage citizens of the U.S. in full- and/or part-time projects designed to combat illiteracy and poverty, provide job skills, enhance educational skills, and fulfill environmental needs. Several provisions are of particular interest to the U.S. Fish and Wildlife Service.

American Conservation and Youth Service Corps: As a federal grant program established under Subtitle C of the law, the Corps offers an opportunity for young adults between the ages of 16–25, or in the case of summer programs, 15–21, to engage in approved human and natural resources projects which benefit the public or are carried out on federal or Indian lands.

To be eligible for assistance, natural resources programs will focus on improvement of wildlife habitat and recreational areas, fish culture, fishery assistance, erosion, wetlands protection, pollution control and similar projects. A stipend of not more than 100 percent of the poverty level will be paid to participants. A Commission established to administer the Youth Service Corps will make grants to states, the Secretaries of Agriculture and Interior and the Director of ACTION to carry out these responsibilities.

Thousand Points of Light: Creates a nonprofit Points of Light Foundation to administer programs to encourage citizens and institutions to volunteer in order to solve critical social issues, and to discover new leaders and develop institutions committed to serving others.

National Historic Preservation Act of 1966 (16 U.S.C. 470–470b, 470c–470n): Public Law 89-665, approved October 15, 1966, (80 Stat. 915) and repeatedly amended, provides for preservation of significant historical features (buildings, objects and sites) through a grant-in-aid program to the states. It establishes a National Register of Historic Places and a program of matching grants under the existing National Trust for Historic Preservation (16 U.S.C. 468–468d).

The act establishes an Advisory Council on Historic Preservation, which was made a permanent independent agency in Public Law 94-422, approved September 28, 1976 (90 Stat. 1319). That act also creates the Historic Preservation Fund. Federal agencies are directed to take into account the effects of their actions on items or sites listed or eligible for listing in the National Register.

As of January 1989, 91 historic sites on national wildlife refuges have been placed on the National Register. There are various laws for the preservation of historic sites and objects:

National Environmental Policy Act of 1969 (P.L. 91-190, 42 U.S.C. 4321–4347, January 1, 1970, 83 Stat. 852) as amended by P.L. 94-52, July 3, 1975, 89 Stat. 258, and P.L. 94-83, August 9, 1975, 89 Stat. 424): Declares

national policy to encourage a productive and enjoyable harmony between humans and their environment. Section 102 of that act directs that "to the fullest extent possible:

- The policies, regulations, and public laws of the United States shall be interpreted and administered in accordance with the policies set forth in this act, and
- All agencies of the federal government shall ... insure that presently unquantified environmental amenities and values may be given appropriate consideration in decision making along with economic technical considerations."

Section 102(2)c of NEPA requires all federal agencies, with respect to major federal actions significantly affecting the quality the quality of the human environment, to submit to the Council on environmental Quality a detailed statement of:

- the environmental impact of the proposed action;
- any adverse environmental effect which cannot be avoided should the proposal be implemented;
- alternatives to the proposed action;
- the relationship between local short-term uses of the environment and the maintenance and enhancement of long-term productivity;
- any irreversible and irretrievable commitments of resources which would be involved in the proposed action, should it be implemented.

National Wildlife Refuge Regulations for the most recent fiscal year (50 CFR 25–35, 43 CFR 3103.2 and 3120.3-3): Provides regulations for administration and management of national wildlife refuges including mineral leasing, exploration, and development.

National Wildlife Refuge System Administration Act of 1966 (Public Law 89-669; 80 Stat. 929; 16 U.S.C. 668dd–668ee), as amended: This act defines the National Wildlife Refuge System as including wildlife refuges, areas for protection and conservation of fish and wildlife which are threatened with extinction, wildlife ranges, game ranges, wildlife management areas, and WPAs. The Secretary is authorized to permit any use of an area provided such use is compatible with the major purposes for which such area was established. The purchase consideration for rights-of-way go into the Migratory Bird Conservation Fund for the acquisition of lands. By regulation, up to 40 percent of an area acquired for a migratory bird sanctuary may be opened to migratory bird hunting unless the Secretary finds that the taking of any species of migratory game birds in more than 40 percent of such area would be beneficial to the species. The act requires an act of Congress for the divestiture of lands in the system, except (1) lands acquired with Migratory Bird Conservation Commission funds, and (2) lands can be removed from the system by land exchange, or if brought into the system by a cooperative agreement, then pursuant to the terms of the agreement.

National Wildlife Refuge System Improvement Act of 1997 (Public Law 105-57, October 9, 1997, Amendment to the National Wildlife Refuge System Administration Act of 1966): This act defines the mission of the National Wildlife Refuge System:

"To administer a national network of lands and waters for the conservation, management, and where appropriate, restoration of the fish, wildlife and plant resources and their habitats within the United States for the benefit of present and future generations of Americans."

Key provisions include the following:

- A requirement that the Secretary of the Interior ensures maintenance of the biological integrity, diversity, and environmental health of the National Wildlife Refuge System;
- The definition of compatible wildlife-dependent recreation as "legitimate and appropriate general public use of the [National Wildlife Refuge] System;"
- The establishment of hunting, fishing, wildlife observation and photography, and environmental education and interpretation as "priority public uses" where compatible with the mission and purpose of individual national wildlife refuges;
- The refuge managers' authority to use sound professional judgment in determining which public uses are

compatible on national wildlife refuge and whether or not they will be allowed (a formal process for determining "compatible use" is currently being developed);
- The requirement of open public involvement in decisions to allow new uses of national wildlife refuges and renew existing ones, as well as in the development of comprehensive conservation plans for national wildlife refuges.

North American Wetlands Conservation Act (103 Stat. 1968; 16 U.S.C. 4401–4412): Public Law 101-233, enacted December 13, 1989, provides funding and administrative direction for implementation of the North American Waterfowl Management Plan and the Tripartite Agreement on wetlands between Canada, U.S. and Mexico.

The act converts the Pittman–Robertson account into a trust fund, with the interest available without appropriation through the year 2006 to carry out the programs authorized by the act, along with an authorization for annual appropriation of $15 million plus an amount equal to the fines and forfeitures collected under the Migratory Bird Treaty Act.

Available funds may be expended, upon approval of the Migratory Bird Conservation Commission, for payment of not to exceed 50 percent of the United States share of the cost of wetlands conservation projects in Canada, Mexico, or the United States (or 100 percent of the cost of projects on federal lands). At least 50 percent and no more than 70 percent of the funds received are to go to Canada and Mexico each year.

Refuge Recreation Act of 1962: Authorizes the Secretary of the Interior to administer refuges, hatcheries, and other conservation areas for recreational use, when such uses do not interfere with the area's primary purposes. It authorizes construction and maintenance of recreational facilities and the acquisition of land for incidental fish and wildlife oriented recreational development or protection of natural resources. It also authorizes the charging of fees for public uses.

Refuge Recreation Act of 1966 (Public Law 87-714; 76 Stat. 653–654; 16 U.S.C. 460k et seq.): Authorizes appropriate, incidental, or secondary recreational use on conservation

areas administered by the Secretary of the Interior for fish and wildlife purposes.

Refuge Revenue Sharing Act (16 U.S.C. 715s): Section 401 of the act of June 15, 1935, (49 Stat. 383) provides for payments to counties in lieu of taxes, using revenues derived from the sale of products from refuges.

Public Law 88-523, approved August 30, 1964, (78 Stat. 701): makes major revisions by requiring that all revenues received from refuge products, such as animals, timber and minerals, or from leases or other privileges, be deposited in a special Treasury account and net receipts distributed to counties for public schools and roads.

Public Law 93-509, approved December 3, 1974, (88 Stat. 1603): requires that moneys remaining in the fund after payments be transferred to the Migratory Bird Conservation Fund for land acquisition under provisions of the Migratory Bird Conservation Act.

Public Law 95-469, approved October 17, 1978, (92 Stat. 1819): expands the revenue sharing system to include National Fish Hatcheries and Service research stations. It also includes in the Refuge Revenue Sharing Fund receipts from the sale of salmonid carcasses. Payments to counties were established as:

1. On acquired land, the greatest amount calculated on the basis of 75 cents per acre, three-fourths of one percent of the appraised value, or 25 percent of the net receipts produced from the land; and

2. On land withdrawn from the public domain, 25 percent of net receipts and basic payments under Public Law 94-565 (31 U.S.C. 1601–1607, 90 Stat. 2662), payment in lieu of taxes on public lands.

This amendment also authorizes appropriations to make up any difference between the amount in the Fund and the amount scheduled for payment in any year. The stipulation that payments be used for schools and roads was removed, but counties were required to pass payments along to other units of local government within the county which

suffer losses in revenues due to the establishment of Service areas.

Refuge Revenue Sharing Act of 1978 (Public Law 95-469, October 17, 1978, [amended 16 U.S.C. 715s]; 50 CFR, part 34): Changes the provisions for sharing revenues with counties in a number of ways. It makes revenue sharing applicable to all lands administered by the Service, whereas previously it was applicable only to areas in the National Wildlife Refuge System. The new law makes payments available for any governmental purpose, whereas the old law restricted the use of payments to roads and schools. For lands acquired in fee simple, the new law provides a payment of 75 cents per acre, 3/4 of 1 percent of fair market value or 25 percent of net receipts, whichever is greatest, whereas the old law provided a payment of 3/4 of 1 percent adjustment cost or 25 percent of net receipts, whichever was greater. The new law makes reserve (public domain) lands entitlement lands under Public Law 94-565 (16 U.S.C. 1601–1607, and provides for a payment of 25 percent of net receipts.

The new law authorizes appropriations to make up any shortfall in net receipts, to make payments in the full amount for which counties are eligible. The old law provided that if net receipts were insufficient to make full payment, payment to each county would be reduced proportionality.

Refuge Trespass Act of June 28, 1906 (18 U.S.C. 41; 43 Stat. 98, 18 U.S.C. 145): Provides first federal protection for wildlife on national wildlife refuges. This act makes it unlawful to hunt, trap, capture, willfully disturb, or kill any bird or wild animal, or take or destroy the eggs of any such birds, on any lands of the United States set apart or reserved as refuges or breeding grounds for such birds or animals by any law, proclamation, or executive order, except under rules and regulations of the Secretary. The act also protects government property on such lands.

Refuge Trespass Act of June 25, 1948 (18 U.S.C. 41. Stat 686)—Section 41 of the Criminal code, title 18: Consolidates the penalty provisions of various acts from January 24, 1905 (16 U.S.C. 684–687; 33 Stat. 614), through March 10, 1934 (16 U.S.C. 694–694b; 48 Stat. 400) and restates the intent of Congress to protect all wildlife within federal sanctuaries, refuges, fish hatcheries and breeding grounds. The act provides that anyone (except in compliance with rules and regulations promulgated by authority of law) who hunts, traps or willfully disturbs any wildlife on such areas, or willfully injures, molest or destroys any property of the United States on such lands or waters, shall be fined, imprisoned, or both.

Rehabilitation Act of 1973 (29 U.S.C. 794), as amended: Title 5 of P.L. 93-112 (87 Stat. 355), signed October 1, 1973, prohibits discrimination on the basis of handicap under any program or activity receiving federal financial assistance.

Rights-of-Way General Regulations (50 CFR 29.21; 34 fr 19907, December 19, 1969): Provides for procedures for filing applications. Provides terms and conditions under which rights-of-way over, above, and across lands administered by the Service may be granted.

Section 401 of the Federal Water Pollution Control Act of 1972 (Public Law 92-500; 86 Stat. 816, 33 U.S.C. 1411): Requires any applicant for a federal license or permit to conduct any activity which may result in a discharge into navigable waters to obtain a certification from the state in which the discharge originates or will originate, or, if appropriate, from the interstate water pollution control agency having jurisdiction over navigable waters at the point where the discharge originates or will originate, that the discharge will comply with applicable effluent limitations and water quality standards. A certification obtained for construction of any facility must also pertain to subsequent operation of the facility.

Section 404 of the Federal Water Pollution Control Act of 1972 (Public Law 92-500, 86 Stat. 816): Authorizes the Secretary of the Army, acting through the Chief of Engineers, to issue permits, after notice and opportunity for public hearing, for discharge of dredged or fill material into navigable waters of the United States, including wetlands, at specified disposal sites. Selection of disposal sites will be in accordance with guidelines developed by the Administrator of the Environmental Protection Agency in conjunction with the Secretary of the Army. Furthermore, the Administrator can prohibit or restrict use of any defined area as a disposal site whenever she/he determines, after notice and opportunity for public hearings, that discharge of such materials into such areas will have an unacceptable adverse effect on municipal water supplies, shellfish beds, fishery areas, wildlife, or recreational areas.

Transfer of Certain Real Property for Wildlife Conservation Purposes Act of 1948: Provides that upon determination by the Administrator of the General Services Administration, real property no longer needed by a federal agency can be transferred, without reimbursement, to the Secretary of the Interior if the land has particular value for migratory birds, or to a state agency for other wildlife conservation purposes.

Wilderness Act of 1964: Public Law 88-577, approved September 3, 1964, directs the Secretary of the Interior, within 10 years, to review every roadless area of 5,000 or more acres and every roadless island (regardless of size) within National Wildlife Refuge and National Park Systems for inclusion in the National Wilderness Preservation System.

Administration of national wildlife refuges is governed by bills passed by the United States Congress and signed into law by the President of the United States, and by regulations promulgated by the various branches of the government. Following is a brief description of some of the most pertinent laws and statues establishing legal parameters and policy direction for the National Wildlife Refuge System:

Wilderness Preservation and Management] (50 CFR 35; 78 Stat. 890; 16 U.S.C. 1131–1136; 43 U.S.C. 1201): Provides procedures for establishing wilderness units under the Wilderness Act of 1964 on units of the National Wildlife Refuge System.

Appendix E. References

Bailey, R.G., Avers, P.E., King, T., and McNab, W.H. (eds.). 1994. Ecoregions and subregions of the United States (map) (supplementary table of map unit descriptions compiled and edited by McNab, W.H. and Bailey, R.G.): Washington, D.C., U.S. Department of Agriculture, Forest Service, scale 1:7,500,000.

Bryce, S., J.M. Omernik, D.E. Pater, M. Ulmer, J. Schaar, J. Freeouf, R. Johnson, P. Kuck, and S.H. Azevedo. 1998. Ecoregions of North Dakota and South Dakota. Jamestown, ND: Northern Prairie Wildlife Research Center Online. http://www.npwrc.usgs.gov/resource /1998/ndsdeco/ndsdeco.htm (Version 30NOV98).

Bureau of Biological Survey. 1939. News release. Twenty Areas in North Dakota Made Refuges for Wildlife.

Cowardin, L.M., V. Carter, F.C. Golet, E.T. LaRoe. 1979. Classification of wetlands and deepwater habitats of the United States. U.S. Department of the Interior, Fish and Wildlife Service, Washington, D.C. Jamestown, ND: Northern Prairie Wildlife Research Center Online. <http://www.npwrc.usgs.gov/resource /1998/classwet/classwet.htm> (Version 04DEC98).

Hendee, C.J. et al. 1990. Wilderness Management. Fulcrum Publishing, North American Press, CO.

Migratory Bird Conservation Commission. 1941. Meeting Minutes. March 25, 1941.

National Wilderness Institute. 1995. State by state government land ownership. <http://www.nwi.org/Maps/LandChart.html>

North Dakota Job Service Data. 2004. Downloaded from: <http://www.jobsnd.com /data/index.html>

North Dakota Legislative Branch. 2005. Maps of Legislative Districts. Downloaded from: <http://web.apps.state.nd.us/hubexplorer/legi slativedist/viewer.html>

Office of Social and Economic Trend Analysis. 2002. Population Estimates 2001–2003. Downloaded from: <http://www.seta.iastate .edu/county/index.aspx?state=ND>

Reynolds, R.E., D.R. Cohan, and C.R. Loesch. 1997. Wetlands of North and South Dakota. Jamestown, ND: Northern Prairie Wildlife

Research Center Home Page. <http://www .npwrc.usgs.gov/resource/othrdata/wetstats/ wetstats.htm> (Version 01OCT97).

Sargeant, A.B., S.H. Allen, and R.T. Eberhardt. 1984. Red fox predation on breeding ducks in mid-continent North America. Wildlife Monographs No. 89, ISSN:0084-0173

Sargeant, Alan B., Raymond J. Greenwood, Marsha A. Sovada, and Terry L. Shaffer. 1993. Distribution and abundance of predators that affect duck production— Prairie Pothole Region. U.S. Fish and Wildlife Service, Resource Publication 194. Jamestown, ND: Northern Prairie Wildlife Research Center Home Page. <http://www .npwrc.usgs.gov/resource/distr/others/predat or/predator.htm>

Sargeant, A.B., M.A. Sovada, and R.J. Greenwood. 1998. Interpreting evidence of depredation of duck nests in the prairie pothole region. U.S. Geological Survey, Northern Prairie Wildlife Research Center, Jamestown, N.D. and Ducks Unlimited, Inc., Memphis, TN. 72 p.

Sargeant, A.B., and D.H. Raveling. 1992. Mortality during the breeding season. Pages 396–422 in B.D.J. Batt, A.D. Afton, M.G. Anderson, C.D. Ankney, D. H. Johnson, J.A. Kadlec, and G.L. Krapu, eds. Ecology and management of breeding waterfowl. Univ. of Minnesota Press, Minneapolis, 635 p.

Sovada, M.A., M.J. Burns, and J.E. Austin. 2001. Predation on waterfowl in arctic tundra and prairie breeding areas: a review. Wildlife Society Bulletin 29(1): 6–15.

Stapp, W.B., et al. (1969). The Concept of Environmental Education. Journal of Environmental Education 1(1): 30–31.

Steen, M.O. Unknown Date (1930s). U.S. Bureau of Biological Survey. Submarginal Migratory Waterfowl Program, North Dakota Easement Projects.

Steen, M.O. Unknown Date (mid-1930s). U.S. Bureau of Biological Survey. Development of Federal Refuges in the Great Plains Region with Emergency Relief Funds.

U.S. Bureau of Census. 2000. United States Census 2000, North Dakota. Downloaded from: <http://www.census.gov/main/www/cen2000.html>

U.S. Department of Agriculture. 2002. USDA Census of Agriculture. Downloaded from: <http://www.nass.usda.gov/census/census02/volume1/nd/st38_2_001_001.pdf>

U.S. Department of Labor. 2005. U.S. Bureau of Labor Statistics Report. Downloaded from: <http://www.bls.gov/>

U.S. Environmental Protection Agency. 2004. Wetlands Overview. EPA 843-F-04-011a, Office of Water. Downloaded from: <http://www.epa.gov/owow/wetlands/pdf/overview.pdf>

U.S. Fish and Wildlife Service. 1998. HAPET and Ducks Unlimited joint venture data.

U.S. Fish and Wildlife Service. 2000. Purposes of the National Wildlife Refuge System Lands. September 27, 2000. Downloaded from: <http://refugedata.fws.gov/databases/purposes.taf?function=form>

U.S. Fish and Wildlife Service. 2000. U.S. Fish and Wildlife Presence in North Dakota. 2000. Downloaded from: <http://mountain-prairie.fws.gov/reference/briefing_book_nd_2000.pdf>

U.S. Fish and Wildlife Service. 2004. National Wetlands Inventory Data.

U.S. Fish and Wildlife Service. 2005. Region 6 Realty Database.

Appendix F. Section 7 Biological Evaluation

MEMORANDUM

To: Refuge Manager, Tewaukon NWR

       Cayuga, North Dakota (Attn: Laura King)

From: Field Supervisor, Ecological Services

       Bismarck, North Dakota

Subject: Review of Draft Comprehensive Conservation Plan and Environmental Assessment for the North Dakota Limited-Interest National Wildlife Refuges

This responds to your recent request for our review of the "Draft Comprehensive Conservation Plan and Environmental Assessment (Plan) for the North Dakota Limited-Interest National Wildlife Refuges (NWR). The draft Plan describes the Refuges' vision for the future, and management goals and objectives in the areas of habitat, wildlife, cultural resources, and wildlife-dependent recreation. The final Plan will guide management of the Refuges for the next 15 years.

A list of federally endangered, threatened, and candidate species and designated critical habitat in North Dakota is enclosed, as requested. This list fulfills requirements of the Fish and Wildlife Service under Section 7 of the Endangered Species Act.

If a Federal agency authorizes, funds, or carries out a proposed action, the responsible Federal agency, or its delegated agent, is required to evaluate whether the action "may affect" listed species or proposed or designated critical habitat. If the Federal agency determines the action "may affect" listed species or proposed or designated critical habitat, then the responsible Federal agency shall request formal section 7 consultation with this office. If the evaluation shows a "no effect" determination for listed species and "no adverse modification" of proposed or designated critical habitat, further consultation is not necessary. If a private entity receives Federal funding for a construction project, or if any Federal permit is required, the Federal agency may designate the fund recipient or permittee as its agent for purposes of section 7 consultation.

A review of our records indicates that the threatened piping plover (*Charadrius melodus*) has been observed at Lake George NWR, which is one of the sites addressed in the draft Plan. A total of 2 piping plover pairs, 3 juveniles, and 1 adult were found at the site in 1993. No other observations have been recorded, likely due to lack of suitable habitat from high water conditions. Lake George NWR was not designated as piping plover critical habitat because it did not meet criteria established by the Fish and Wildlife Service (i.e., breeding piping plovers observed in more than 1 year for the period of survey record). No sites addressed in the draft Plan have been designated as piping plover critical habitat.

Confirmed sightings of the endangered whooping crane (*Grus americana*) during spring or fall migration are known from 5 sites addressed in the draft Plan, as follows:

Limited-Interest NWR	Date	Number of Adults	Number of Juveniles	Total
Dakota Lake	10-16-90	2	0	2
Lake Patricia	4-10-00	6	0	6
Pretty Rock	10-28-85	6	1	7
Pretty Rock	10-16-02	6	1	7
Pretty Rock	11-2-04	2	0	2
Sheyenne Lake	4-11-85	5	0	5
Willow Lake	4-15-98	5	0	5

Thank you for coordinating your draft Plan with our office. If additional information is required, please contact Karen Kreil of my staff or myself at 701-250-4481 or at the letterhead address.

Attachments

FEDERAL THREATENED, ENDANGERED, AND CANDIDATE SPECIES

AND DESIGNATED CRITICAL HABITAT FOUND IN

NORTH DAKOTA

December 2005

ENDANGERED SPECIES

Birds

Interior least tern (Sterna antillarum): Nests along midstream sandbars of the Missouri and Yellowstone Rivers.

Whooping crane (Grus Americana): Migrates through west and central counties during spring and fall. Prefers to roost on wetlands and stockdams with good visibility. Young adult summered in North Dakota in 1989, 1990, and 1993. Total population 140–150 birds.

Fish

Pallid sturgeon (Scaphirhynchus albus): Known only from the Missouri and Yellowstone Rivers. No reproduction has been documented in 15 years.

Mammals

Black-footed ferret (Mustela nigripes): Exclusively associated with prairie dog towns. No records of occurrence in recent years, although there is potential for reintroduction in the future.

Gray wolf (Canis lupus): Occasional visitor in North Dakota. Most frequently observed in the Turtle Mountains area.

THREATENED SPECIES

Birds

Bald eagle (Haliaeetus leucocephalus): Migrates spring and fall statewide but primarily along the major river courses. It concentrates along the Missouri River during winter and is known to nest in the floodplain forest.

Piping plover (Charadrius melodus): Nests on midstream sandbars of the Missouri and Yellowstone Rivers and along shorelines of saline wetlands. More nest in North Dakota than any other state.

Plants

W. prairie-fringed orchid (Platanthera praeclara): Locally common in moist swales on Sheyenne National Grasslands. Largest known U.S. population is on the Sheyenne.

CANDIDATE SPECIES

Invertebrates

Dakota skipper (Hesperia dacotae): Found in native prairie containing a high diversity of wildflowers and grasses. Habitat includes two prairie types: 1) low (wet) prairie dominated by bluestem grasses, wood lily, harebell, and smooth camas; 2) upland (dry) prairie on ridges and hillsides dominated by bluestem grasses, needlegrass, pale purple and upright coneflowers and blanketflower.

DESIGNATED CRITICAL HABITAT

Birds

Piping Plover - Alkali Lakes and Wetlands - Critical habitat includes: (1) shallow, seasonally to permanently flooded, mixosaline to hypersaline wetlands with sandy to gravelly, sparsely vegetated beaches, salt-encrusted mud flats, and/or gravelly salt flats; (2) springs and fens along edges of alkali lakes and wetlands; and (3) adjacent uplands 200 feet (61 meters) above the high water mark of the alkali lake or wetland.

Piping Plover - Missouri River - Critical habitat includes sparsely vegetated channel sandbars, sand and gravel beaches on islands, temporary pools on sandbars and islands, and the interface with the river.

Piping Plover - Lake Sakakawea and Oahe - Critical habitat includes sparsely vegetated shoreline beaches, peninsulas, islands composed of sand, gravel, or shale, and their interface with the water bodies.

County Occurrence of Endangered, Threatened and Candidate Species and Designated Critical Habitat in North Dakota March 2005 through December 2005

Species	Adams	Barnes	Benson	Billings	Bottineau	Bowman	Burke	Burleigh	Cass	Cavalier	Dickey	Divide	Dunn	Eddy	Emmons	Foster	Go Valley	Gr. Forks	Grant	Griggs	Hettinger	Kidder	Lamoure	Logan	McHenry	McIntosh	McKenzie
Interior Least Tern - E	X							X					X		X												X
Whooping Crane - E	X	X		X	X	X	X	X		X	X	X	X	X	X	X	X		X	X	X	X	X	X	X	X	X
Black-footed Ferret - E	X			X		X							X				X		X		X						X
Pallid Sturgeon - E								X					X		X												X
Gray Wolf - E		X			X		X	X	X	X	X	X	X					X							X	X	X
Bald Eagle - T	X	X	X	X	X	X	X	X	X	X	X	X	X	X	X	X	X	X	X	X	X	X	X	X	X	X	X
Piping Plover - T			X				X	X				X	X	X	X	X						X		X	X	X	X
Western Prairie Fringed Orchid - T																											
Dakota Skipper - C							X							X											X		X
Designated Critical Habitat																											
Piping Plover	X						X	X				X	X	X	X							X		X	X	X	X

E = Endangered; T = Threatened; C = Candidate

County Occurrence of Endangered, Threatened and Candidate Species and Designated Critical Habitat in North Dakota March 2005 through December 2005

Species	McLean	Mercer	Morton	Mountrail	Nelson	Oliver	Pembina	Pierce	Ramsey	Ranson	Renville	Richland	Rolette	Sargent	Sheridan	Sioux	Slope	Stark	Steele	Stutsman	Towner	Traill	Walsh	Ward	Wells	Williams
Interior Least Tern – E	X	X	X	X		X										X										X
Whooping Crane – E	X	X	X	X		X		X			X	X	X		X	X	X	X		X	X			X	X	X
Black-footed Ferret – E	X	X	X			X										X	X	X								
Pallid Sturgeon – E	X	X	X	X		X										X										X
Gray Wolf – E	X	X	X	X	X	X	X	X	X		X	X	X	X	X	X	X	X	X	X	X	X	X	X	X	X
Bald Eagle - T	X	X	X	X	X	X	X	X	X	X	X	X	X	X	X	X	X	X	X	X	X	X	X	X	X	X
Piping Plover - T	X	X	X	X		X		X			X		X	X	X	X				X		X	X	X	X	X
W. P. Fringed Orchid – T										X		X														
Dakota Skipper - C										X		X	X	X						X				X		
Designated Critical Habitat																										
Piping Plover	X	X	X	X		X		X							X	X				X				X		X

E = Endangered; T = Threatened; C = Candidate

United States Department of the Interior

FISH AND WILDLIFE SERVICE
Mountain-Prairie Region

IN REPLY REFER TO: MAILING ADDRESS:
Tewaukon National Wildlife Refuge
9754 143 ½ Ave. SE
Cayuga, ND 58013

January 11, 2006

To: Jeffrey Towner, Field Supervisor, Ecological Services
Bismarck, North Dakota

From: Laura King, Planning Team Leader
Cayuga, North Dakota

Subject: Section 7 consultation for the North Dakota Limited-interest National Wildlife Refuge Comprehensive Conservation Plan

This memo is to request your concurrence of a 'no effect' determination for the actions proposed in the North Dakota Limited-interest National Wildlife Refuges Comprehensive Conservation Plan (CCP).

Based on the information provided by your office, we don't feel that any action in this plan will affect endangered species or proposed or designated critical habitat. According to Service data, there is no suitable habitat on any of these 39 refuges for such federally listed species such as pallid sturgeon, black-footed ferret, or least tern. Our refuges located near the Turtle Mountain area, an area known for wolf dispersal, do not have the habitat needed to sustain wolf populations. Bald eagles may pass through these refuges during migration, but no refuge contains significant riparian habitat, the preferred habitat of bald eagles. The Dakota skipper is a candidate species known to occur in North Dakota; however there are no records of Dakota skipper on lands included in the ND Limited-interest CCP. Regardless, the activities proposed in this plan would not impact any of these species but rather are generally consistent with recovery of these candidate, threatened, and endangered animals.

Piping plovers were identified on Lake George NWR. However, this occurrence was one year only and therefore is not designated as piping plover critical habitat. Even though the goals in this plan support piping plover recovery, the refuges will consult with Ecological Services on any future management at this site that may affect the piping plover.

Migrating whooping cranes have been identified at five of the refuges in this project. However, these occurrences are sporadic with either single sightings or with two to seven years between occurrences. Although the actions proposed in this plan support whooping crane recovery, the refuges will consult with Ecological Services on any future management actions that may affect whooping cranes.

We appreciated you assistance in completing this consultation. If additional information is needed, please contact me at Tewaukon NWR at 701-724-3598 (ext. *814).

United States Department of the Interior

FISH AND WILDLIFE SERVICE
Ecological Services
3425 Miriam Avenue
Bismarck, North Dakota 58501

JAN 2 6 2006

MEMORANDUM

To: Planning Team Leader, Tewaukon NWR
        Cayuga, North Dakota

From: Field Supervisor, Ecological Services
        Bismarck, North Dakota

Subject: Intra-Service Section 7 Consultation - North Dakota Limited-interest National Wildlife
        Refuge Comprehensive Conservation Plan

I am writing in response to your January 11, 2006, request for our concurrence with your
threatened and endangered species effect determination relative to the subject Comprehensive
Conservation Plan. We have reviewed the information provided and concur with your
determination of no effect for whooping crane, gray wolf, bald eagle, Dakota skipper, piping
plover, and piping plover critical habitat. If you have any questions regarding this informal
consultation, please contact Karen Kreil of my staff at 701-355-8506, or contact me directly at
(701)250-4402, extension 508, or at the letterhead address.

Appendix G. Divestiture Model

I. Introduction

The divestiture model represents a set of criteria for measuring the value of a refuge. Designed as a pre-planning tool, the model allows planners and refuge managers to determine whether or not a refuge should be considered for divestiture. If the model indicates that a refuge should be considered for divestiture, the process and consequences of divestiture will be studied further during the CCP process. Six of the 39 refuges were recommended for divestiture following these criteria.

II. The Divestiture Model – Criteria and Rules

Region 6's divestiture model was developed during a two day workshop held December 14–15, 2004 by a team of refuge managers, biologists, planner, and the Regional Office directorate. The purpose of the workshop was to standardize policy in Region 6 for identifying which refuges to consider for divestiture. The Service recognizes that this is very significant decision and that divestiture will always be the exception and not the rule. However, in a 100 year history of establishing refuges, there may be instances, such as in the case of the North Dakota Limited-interest Program, where refuges no longer support the mission and goals of the National Wildlife Refuge System. These refuges may be draining resources from those areas with greater potential.

The model consists of a set of eight questions that must be addressed when considering a refuge for divestiture. The questions were prioritized as primary and secondary criteria for evaluation.

A. Primary Criteria

1. Does the refuge achieve one or more of the NWRS goals?
Explanation: Look beyond the purpose to see if the refuge is meeting NWRS goals. Refuge purpose is forever, but may become obsolete over time (e.g. recovery of T&E species). Obsolete purpose doesn't necessarily mean we should get rid of the refuge.

2. Does the refuge meet its purpose (fulfill the refuge's intent and statutory purpose)?
Explanation: Try to understand the intent of decision makers at the time the refuge was established.

3. Does the refuge provide substantial support for migratory bird species, provide important sheltering habitat for threatened and endangered species, or support species identified in authorizing legislation?
Explanation: The planning team that answers this question must define 'substantial.' Refuge context is the key consideration. Substantial is relative to species, location, region etc.
Example: Flocks of migratory birds (thousands) would be considered substantial.

4A. Does the refuge have biological integrity; if not, is it feasible to restore the biological integrity of the converted or degraded habitat?
Explanation: The presence of native habitat is not enough to meet NWRS standard; USFWS is not trying to save every remnant species. Identify what has changed from presettlement habitat conditions. Consider the contribution to regional biodiversity.

4B. Does the Service have or can it reasonably acquire the right to restore the habitat?
Biological integrity = native habitat and contribution to regional biodiversity.
Degraded = Native vegetation exists but the value has been reduced due to nonnatives and loss of ecological functions.

*In order to answer "yes" on biological integrity need to answer yes on both "4A" and "4B"

5. Does it contribute to landscape conservation, provide a stepping stone for migratory birds or serve as a unique habitat patch important to the conservation of a Trust species?

B. Secondary Criteria

6. Politics/Community – Is there such significant community interest in and support for the refuge that divesture would result in unacceptable long-term public relations?
Explanation: Environmental education is a means to an end; not a purpose in itself; conservation must be broader than refuge. Public Use should be considered as criteria only when public use is legislated in the purpose.

7. Jurisdiction – Do we have or can we acquire the jurisdiction to meet refuge's purpose, NWRS mission and goals, and prevent incompatible uses?

8. Other Land Manager - Can someone else achieve most or all of the purposes of the refuge without the Service having to incurring costs?
(This question is very relative to these limited-interest refuges where the Service in essence remains in name only, e.g. Sheyenne Lake NWR. Three of the six refuges proposed for divestiture are either owned and/or being managed by the state)

C. Additional Considerations

9. Cost/Liability – Cost will never be a primary or secondary factor for divesting a refuge; cost (in itself) should not be a criterion for divesting land.
- If cost is a consideration for divestiture, it is because some other factor is driving the decision.
- Treat cost as a piece of information that can be used to justify decision
- Liability is an additive to a decision to either keep or divest a refuge, but it is not a primary or secondary decision making criteria.

D. Rules – *The following five rules organize the responses to the above criteria questions and determine whether or not to consider a refuge for divestiture.*

Rule 1: IF the refuge cannot meet one or more NWRS goals, THEN it should be considered for divestiture.

Rule 2: IF the answers to questions 1–4 are as follows,
1. Yes – Meets a NWRS goal, but only the education goal
2. No – Does not meet refuge purpose
3. No – Does not substantially support trust species
4. No – Does not possess biological integrity
THEN the refuge should be considered for divestiture.

Rule 3: IF the answers to questions 1–5 are as follows,
1. Yes – Meets a NWRS goal, but only the education goal
2. Yes - Purpose
3. No – Trust Species
4. No – Biological Integrity
5. No – Connectivity
THEN the refuge should be considered for divestiture.

Rule 4: IF the answers to questions 1–6 are as follows,
1. Yes – Goal
2. Maybe – Purpose
3. No – Trust Species
4. Yes – Biological Integrity
5. No – Connectivity

6. Yes – Jurisdiction
THEN keep the refuge (positive rule).

Rule 5: IF the answers to questions 1–3 are as follows,
1. Yes – Goal
2. Yes – Purpose
3. Yes – Trust Species
THEN keep the refuge (positive rule).

Summary

What is this document? This is the comprehensive conservation plan and environmental assessment for the North Dakota Limited-interest National Wildlife Refuges Program. This comprehensive conservation plan is based on the best available science (see "Appendix E, References") and will guide the management of these 39 limited-interest refuges for the next 15 years.

What is a limited-interest refuge? The Service has limited capabilities on these refuges (see section 2.3). Most agreements include the right to manage water uses, hunting, and trapping on the refuges.

Who completed this plan? The U.S. Fish and Wildlife Service and the North Dakota Game and Fish Department, under the guidance of the Region 6, Mountain-Prairie Region, Division of Refuge Planning. This interdisciplinary team (see appendix A) spent over a year and a half planning and meeting and listening to the public's ideas and concerns prior to preparing this document.

Why did the Service complete this comprehensive conservation plan and environmental assessment? In 1997, Congress passed the National Wildlife Refuge System Improvement Act legislation, which provides clear guidance for the management of the National Wildlife Refuge System. The act included a new statutory mission statement (see section 1.2) and directed the Service to manage the refuge system as a national system of lands and waters devoted to conserving wildlife and maintaining biological integrity of ecosystems.

In order to support and fulfill this mission, this act also required that by 2012, the U.S. Fish and Wildlife Service will have developed a comprehensive conservation plan for each national wildlife refuge in the System at the time of the act. This includes these 39 refuges in this comprehensive conservation plan.

Why did you address 39 refuges in one plan? These refuges are unique among all other national wildlife refuges. Even though the North Dakota Limited-interest Refuge Program began almost 70 years ago, today 99 percent of the lands within the approved acquisition boundaries remain in private ownership. The Service has limited capabilities on these refuges (see section 2.3) and the habitat is similar amongst these refuges. In particular, most have a water feature, such as a lake, river, or impoundment, which was a major focus of the limited-interest refuge agreement and designated boundaries. No approved guidelines have been established for managing this program. Given these facts, the planning team felt it was more effective to address the issues and future of these refuges as a program through a programmatic comprehensive conservation plan rather than as individual plans.

Where are these refuges located? All but two (Lake Patricia and Pretty Rock NWRs) of the 39 refuges are located east of the Missouri River from the Canadian to South Dakota Borders (see figure 2).

How large are these refuges? They range in size from 160 acres (Half Way Lake) to 5,500 acres (Rock Lake). There are 47,296 acres of limited-interest refuge acres within the 54,140-acre approved acquisition boundaries. The approved acquisition boundaries were established by executive order or other legislation in the 1930s and 1940s. Not all acres within this approved acquisition boundary are covered by a Service limited-interest refuge.

What is the history and purpose of the North Dakota Limited-interest Refuge Program? The North Dakota Limited-interest Refuge Program began in the 1930s, in response to the many crises of the "Dust Bowl Era." Working with states and private landowners, Roosevelt established the North Dakota Limited-interest Refuge Program for purpose of "drought relief, water conservation, and for migratory bird and wildlife conservation." Hundreds of landowners agreed to place their lands under this program, most perpetual, for these conservation purposes. Dozens of easement agreements were signed by landowners in North Dakota.

The economic crisis of this era was also addressed through this program. Local communities were put back to work through the Works Progress/Project Administration and Civilian Conservation Corps, federal job programs used to build structures to impound and control water on these limited-interest refuge lands. This water provided landowners with critical stock water while migrating waterfowl and other waterbirds benefited from this reliable water source and sanctuary.

Although most were perpetually protected, a new status was given to these lands in the late 1930s and '40s. Refuge lands in close proximity were combined and designated as Migratory Bird Sanctuaries (later changed to national wildlife refuges) under the authorities of executive orders and conservation laws.

What is the vision for the North Dakota Limited-interest Refuge Program?
Since our Nation's beginning, great flocks of wildfowl—ducks, geese and waterbirds—provided sights and sounds, food and feather. These wings of migration not only inspired hunters but some of our greatest artists, photographers, and poets. In the 1930s, much of the United States, including North Dakota, was gripped by a devastating drought and depression. Hot winds that dried crops also dried wetlands. Wildfowl numbers plummeted, and the skies grew quiet.

Americans took this crisis and saw opportunity and a great partnership was formed. Conservation leaders, the State of North Dakota, the federal government, and private landowners laid the foundation for what would become the North Dakota Limited-interest Refuge Program. This Program addressed both wildlife conservation and economic needs. The Works Progress/Program Administration and Civilian Conservation Corps brought jobs to the communities building dams and other structures to create water areas that now provide habitat and sanctuary for waterfowl and other migratory birds.

Through cooperation with the current refuge landowners and other conservation partners, the Program will realize its full potential. It will become a premier example of private land partnerships promoting fish and wildlife conservation, supporting other conservation programs while continuing to serve as sanctuaries for international migratory birds.

What goals does the Service hope to accomplish to achieve this vision?

Goal 1. Wetland Habitat: Maintain and manage natural and created wetlands within the approved acquisition boundary to provide habitat for international populations of waterfowl and other migratory birds along with other wetland-dependent wildlife.

Goal 2. Upland Habitat: Establish a land protection program within the approved acquisition boundary to maintain, restore, and enhance uplands to provide habitat for international populations of waterfowl, other migratory birds, and other wildlife.

Goal 3. Partnerships: Foster beneficial landowner, community, and regional partnerships to assist in achieving the Program vision while ensuring 100 percent of all partners gain a greater understanding of the management and resources of the limited-interest refuges.

Goals 4. Visitor Services: Where compatible, and in cooperation with willing landowners, allow public fishing, hunting, trapping, and other high quality wildlife-dependent recreation opportunities that foster an appreciation and understanding of the management and resources of the North Dakota Limited-interest Refuge Program and the National Wildlife Refuge System.

Goal 5. Administration: Secure and effectively utilize funding, staffing, and partnerships to ensure the Program meets its full potential of habitat protection and visitor use.

Will any of the actions proposed in this plan be completed without landowner concurrence? No action outside the authority of the limited-interest refuge agreement as outlined in section 2.3 of this document will be conducted without full coordination and cooperation of willing landowners. If a landowner does not wish to participate in a program outside the authority of the limited-interest refuge agreement, the landowner may do so without retribution and may, at any time, contact the Service should the landowner change his or her mind.

What alternatives did the Service evaluate?
The no-action alternative (current management) and the preferred alternative

(enhance the program). Because there have never been any approved guidelines for this program and these refuges, the only viable action that could be considered in this programmatic CCP is some form of enhancement, as outlined below and in chapter 6.

What are some of the key actions outlined in the preferred alternative?

- Divestiture of six refuges due to significant loss of biodiversity and ownership patterns (i.e., lands owned and/or managed for wildlife by another federal or state agency). These refuges include:

  - Bone Hill NWR—significant loss of biodiversity and development

  - Camp Lake NWR—significant loss of biodiversity and development

  - Cottonwood Lake NWR—significant loss of biodiversity and development

  - Lake Patricia—majority of lands owned/managed by the state

  - Sheyenne Lake NWR—owned/managed by Bureau of Reclamation

  - School Section Lake NWR—majority of lands owned/managed by the state

- Each managing station will actively share information and engage landowners in the management of these refuges and the implementation of the final comprehensive conservation plan.

- Evaluate all existing structures and determine the maintenance and replacement needs necessary to properly manage water levels on refuge impoundments.

- Each managing station will evaluate and prioritize its limited-interest refuges to ensure the most critical wetland and upland habitats are protected.

  - Highest priority will be given to those refuges with native prairie habitat

- Work with willing landowners to provide additional compensation for added habitat protections through various programs including conservation partner programs, compensated easement programs, and fee-title acquisitions.

  - Develop partnerships with other state, federal, and conservation organizations to achieve common goals that enhance and support the North Dakota Limited-interest Refuge Program.

- Continue existing visitor services programs, where appropriate, and work with willing landowners and the North Dakota Game and Fish Department to determine if there are additional opportunities to accommodate the six priority public uses.

- Recruit one state coordinator for the North Dakota Limited-interest Refuge Program to work with landowners and oversee the implementation this comprehensive conservation plan.

Which alternative did the Service choose for the final CCP?

Alternative B (enhance the program) was selected by the regional director because it best meets the purposes for which these refuges were established and is preferable to the no-action alternative in light of physical, biological, economic, and social factors. (See "Appendix C, Decision Documents.")

What happens next?

The Service will now begin to implement the plan and continue to do so over the next 15 years, when it will be revised. It is important to note that some of the objectives and strategies (see chapter 6) require a substantial increase in current funding. The Service will pursue these additional resources but there is no guarantee of funding increases and therefore no guarantee that all actions identified will be completed within the life of this plan. However, for the first time in 70 years, the issues that have impeded these limited-interest refuges have been elevated to all levels in the Service while giving managers the first long-term guidance for management decisions and setting priorities on these refuges.